THE CATHOLIC READER'S BIBLE

◆ ◆

The Epistles and Revelation

THE CATHOLIC READER'S BIBLE

◆ ◆

The Epistles and Revelation

Sophia Institute Press
Manchester, New Hampshire

Nihil Obstat
Rt. Rev. Msgr. Henry J. Grimmelsman, S.T.D.
Rev. John F. McConnell, M.M., S.T.L., S.S.L.
Rev. Joseph J. Tennant, S.T.D., S.S.L.

Imprimatur
Most Rev. Thomas H. McLaughlin, S.T.D., Bishop of Paterson

A Revision of the Challoner-Rheims Version
Edited by Catholic scholars under the patronage of the
Episcopal Committee of the Confraternity of Christian Doctrine
Translated from the Latin Vulgate

The Catholic Reader's Bible: The Epistles and Revelation
Copyright © 2020 Sophia Institute

Printed in the United States of America. All rights reserved.

Cover design:
Cover image:

Sophia Institute Press
Box 5284, Manchester, NH 03108
1-800-888-9344
www.SophiaInstitute.com
Sophia Institute Press® is a registered trademark of Sophia Institute.

ISBN 978-1-64413-323-1
eBook ISBN 978-1-64413-324-8
Library of Congress Control Number:

First printing

Contents

CONTENTS

REVELATION

Foreword to the Confraternity Revision of the New Testament

By Most Rev. Amleto Giovanni Cicognani
Apostolic Delegate to the United States

"The excellent revision of the Rheims-Douay Version of the Scriptures made in 1750 by Bishop Challoner, Vicar Apostolic of the London District, is an admirable accomplishment. This work had become in many respects obsolete and unintelligible in its archaic expressions. A new revision meant an analytical, critical, and literary work of such magnitude that to attempt it seemed not only a risk but almost a dream. The revision of the New Testament is now a happy reality and has won the applause of the most competent scholars. Study for the revision continued over more than five years, under the direction of about thirty Biblical scholars from among the clergy, generously assisted by the active members of the Catholic Biblical Association of America. The names of these scholars have very appropriately been listed on the last page of the new volume of the New Testament as a tribute of undying gratitude. . . .

"The New Testament is the code of love and salvation. It carries the Word of God, the revelation of our Lord through His teachings. It is of utmost importance, for every age, not least for our own, to hear it with the same clarity, vividness, and comprehension with which it was first pronounced by our Lord.

"Search the Scriptures (cf. John 5:39). They have been given 'for our instruction, that through . . . the consolation afforded by the Scriptures we may have hope' (Romans 15:4)."

Excerpts from the address to the Seventh National Congress of the Confraternity of Christian Doctrine, Philadelphia, November 16, 1941, reproduced here with the approval of His Excellency the Apostolic Delegate.

"On the Reading of Holy Scripture" from the Encyclical Letter *Spiritus Paraclitus* of Pope Benedict XV (September 15, 1920)

"Since the Holy Spirit, the Comforter, had bestowed the Scriptures on the human race for their instruction in Divine things, He also raised up in successive ages saintly and learned men whose task it should be to develop that treasure and so provide for the faithful plenteous 'consolation afforded by the Scriptures' (Romans 15:4). Foremost among these teachers stands St. Jerome. . . . The responsibility of our Apostolic office impels us to set before you his wonderful example and so promote the study of Holy Scripture in accordance with the teachings of our predecessors, Leo XIII and Pius X.

"And none can fail to see what profit and sweet tranquillity must result in well-disposed souls from such devout reading of the Bible. Whoever comes to it in piety, faith, and humility, and with a determination to make progress in it, will assuredly find therein and will eat the 'bread that comes down from heaven' (John 6:50).

"Hence, as far as in us lies, we, Venerable Brethren, shall, with St. Jerome as our guide, never desist from urging the faithful to read daily the Gospels, the Acts, and the Epistles, so as to gather thence food for their souls. . . . But what, in his view, is the goal of such study? First, that from the Bible's pages we learn spiritual perfection. . . . Secondly, it is from the Bible that we gather confirmations and illustrations of any particular doctrine we wish to defend. . . . We confidently hope that his example will fire both clergy and laity with enthusiasm for the study of the Bible. . . . So convinced indeed was Jerome that familiarity with the Bible was the royal road to the knowledge and love of Christ that he did not hesitate to say: 'Ignorance of the Bible means ignorance of Christ' ('Prol. in Comment. in Isa.'; cf. 'Tract. de Ps. 77').

"Jerome still calls to us. His voice rings out, telling us of the super-excellence of Holy Scripture, of its integral character and historical trustworthiness, telling us, too, of the pleasant fruits resulting from reading and meditating upon it.

"Our one desire for all the Church's children is that, being saturated with the Bible, they may arrive at the all-surpassing knowledge of Jesus Christ."

Pope Leo XIII granted to the faithful who shall read for at least a quarter of an hour the books of the Sacred Scripture with the veneration due to the Divine Word and as spiritual reading, an indulgence of 300 days.

—*Preces et Pia Opera*, 645

Preface

"The word of the Lord endures forever," is the saying of a great prophet (Isaiah 40:8) and of the Prince of the Apostles (1 Peter 1:25).

In her belief in the divine authority and the perfect truth of the Bible, as being the inspired Word of God, the Catholic Church has never hesitated. Nor has the Church forgotten that this sacred Book was destined by its Author to convey His message to all His faithful servants of every place and time. Neither has she overlooked the fact that this message must lie sealed and silent to many of her children unless given them in their own language, at least by the voice of their pastors, if not by means of the written page.

Further, the Church has always realized that Holy Scripture was committed to her charge by virtue of its very origin and object. Like the Apostolic Tradition of Christ's teaching, the Bible, too, is a treasury of divine revelation. As such, it can have no rightful guardian and dispenser except that Church which Christ formed and commissioned to teach to all the world the truths revealed for man's salvation. There can be no graver crime than the least corruption of that eternal truth which Christ has brought us. The Church is, therefore, watchful over Holy Scripture; and not only over its message, but likewise over its written transmission.

In exercising this guardianship, the Church has given special sanction to that Latin version which, because of its common use for centuries, won the name of "Vulgate." Her intention in this is primarily to declare which of many Latin versions is to be regarded as substantially accurate and safe in all matters of faith and morals. It was from this Latin text that most of the vernacular versions of Europe were made. It was also from this text that our first printed Catholic Bible in English was taken.

In 1560 the Catholic Church had been outlawed in England. The Catholics who remained in the country faced a particular danger to their faith from English versions of the Bible which altered the true meaning of the Scriptures. To meet this danger there was urgent need of a more faithful, a Catholic, version. This need was met by the "Rheims and Douay Version." It was so called because the New Testament was printed at Rheims in 1582, and the Old Testament at Douay in 1609–10. It was the work of exiled English priests and educators, the chief of whom was Dr. Gregory Martin.

The Rheims-Douay remained the standard English version for Catholic use until near the time of the American Revolution. By this time the language had passed through many of those changes which are natural to all living tongues. It was Bishop Challoner, Vicar Apostolic of the London District, who saw the pressing need of an English version of the Bible more in keeping with the time. In spite of his heavy pastoral labors, he produced a new version of the entire Bible in English in 1750. Challoner regarded his work as merely a revision of the Rheims-Douay, as its title page shows. The Catholic version in English that is best known to us all, both in England and in America, is still practically that of Challoner. Other Catholic scholars sought to improve on his work, and some of our current editions are indebted to them as well; but Challoner's Bible has been the framework and the substance of our own down to the present time.

But, in its turn, Challoner's version has suffered loss of value because of progressive changes in our language. The consequent need of revision in which it stands has been recognized for a long time. Challoner's text was made the approved English version for Catholics in America by the Archbishop of Baltimore and the Bishops of the United States in 1810. The approbation was confirmed by the Hierarchy at the First Provincial Council of Baltimore (1829), but at the same time the emendation of the "Douay" text, as Challoner's was still described, was earnestly recommended. This matter of the improvement of Challoner's version came up again at the Ninth Provincial Council of Baltimore (1858). The Sacred Congregation *de Propaganda Fide* sanctioned in a particular way this desire for a better vernacular version, suggesting that it be entrusted to a group of theologians experienced in biblical studies.

Notwithstanding this encouragement to undertake a revision of the approved version, the closing decades of the last century, and the first of the present century, found the Church in America too much occupied with other concerns and not sufficiently equipped to attempt this work. Archbishop Kenrick undertook the great task of revising the entire Bible, but his work never met with general acceptance.

The result was that we have continued to use editions of the English Bible which are, in language and substance, the text that Bishop Challoner gave us 190 years ago.

The passage of time has neither lessened the weaknesses of this version nor done away with the demand for its improvement. In the meantime, however, the number of priests in America trained in the theological sciences, and notably in the specialized discipline of biblical studies, has greatly increased. Parallel to this growth there has been a marked increase of popular interest in the study of Holy Scripture. This progress has brought to light again the unsatisfactory condition of our vernacular version; it has reawakened the desire for a version accommodated to the needs of our time; and it has called attention to the fact that we now possess the adequate means to produce a worthy English text.

The English version which is presented in this volume is the answer of the Church in America to this need. Its preparation was requested and supervised by the Episcopal Committee of the Confraternity of Christian Doctrine. The principles upon which it rests were submitted to the Secretary and to other members of the Biblical Commission at Rome and received complete approval. It is the accomplishment of some twenty-seven Catholic biblical scholars, all men of training and experience in their particular field, who have devoted more than five years to the work. Many other scholars have had part in it, whether as special editors or as critics. It enjoys, therefore, in the first place the authority necessary in any serious attempt to meet the requirements of an improved Catholic version in English. And it claims a scholarship commensurate with that authority.

While new in many of its aspects, this text is not a new

version, but a revision of the work done by Bishop Challoner. While that venerable text has lost a great deal of its value with the lapse of time, it retains much that is commendable. To produce the type of version required in our day, it was necessary to eliminate many of the characteristics of the older version, and even to change many of its familiar passages; but there was no reason for setting it aside entirely. In fact, this revised text can claim the advantage of preserving in an improved form the version to which English-speaking Catholics have become accustomed.

The English text now being presented retains as much as possible of the version it seeks to replace. And yet, in striving for expression that is modern, much of the general style of Challoner's work has been improved upon. Many terms found in his version are no longer current in the sense in which he used them. The close adherence to Latin sentence structure, so evident in his text, is not the usage of our time. Such modifications are inevitable. It may be stated, however, that only such alterations in the Challoner text have been made in the revised edition as were necessary to give a simple and clear modern version.

However, this present text is much more than an effort to bring the language of Challoner's version into conformity with modern English idiom. It is a revision in the sense that it goes back to the source upon which Challoner drew, and it reconsiders in a thorough way the accurate rendering of the divine message in the language of our day.

Like both the Rheims and the Challoner versions, the revised text rests upon the Latin Vulgate. This has been made necessary by a desire to have the version available for liturgical use. The excellence of the Vulgate as an ancient interpretation of the New Testament is an added advantage. The Clementine edition of the Vulgate is the main source of this revision. The readings of the Clementine, however, have been improved in not a few instances by recourse to the witnesses for a more ancient text of the Vulgate. This tends to bring the text basic to the present version very close to the modem critical editions of the original Greek.

One immediate influence of the Vulgate will be observed in the spelling of proper names. The Latin form has been retained as more familiar to Catholics, and in some instances closer to the original pronunciation.

In addition to improving on Challoner's use of the Latin text, the revised version will show the results of a more thorough method of interpretation. The Latin text often reflects the peculiarities and idiom of its Semitic and Greek origin. In accordance with the rules of sound biblical interpretation, the present version takes this into account; and when the Latin text clearly supposes such elements, it renders them in the sense that is native to them. In no case, however, has the Latin text been set side in favor of the Greek. It can, therefore, be said that the present version is in every sense a translation of the Vulgate.

As a further aid to the reading and understanding of the divine message, this new text abandons the old verse form of Challoner for the still older paragraphing of the Rheims-Douay Bible. Another improvement is offered in the addition of headings that show the main divisions of the books, and titles describing the contents of their subdivisions.

This revised version is presented with the confidence that it will advance the reading and appreciation of the New

Testament. It is offered with the hope that it may awaken new interest in the Word of God, and that it may bring to God's children the manifold blessings of His Letter to them. At the same time, it is presented with the humble prayer that, as it has been prepared with all diligence and care, it may not interpret the divine message in any way except in the full sense intended by the Holy Spirit. It is He who has given it to us for our instruction, and that we may have hope (Romans 15:4).

The Life and Epistles of St. Paul

St. Paul was born at Tarsus, Cilicia, of Jewish parents who were descended from the tribe of Benjamin (Acts 9:11; 21:39; 22:3). He was a Roman citizen from birth (Acts 22:27f). As he was "a young man" at the stoning of St. Stephen (Acts 7:58) and calls himself "an old man" when writing to Philemon (v. 9), about the year 63, we may conclude that he was born around the beginning of the Christian era.

In his youth Paul acquired a threefold education. First, he learned the Greek language in his Tarsian environment, as is evident from his later skill in writing his Epistles. Secondly, his father probably initiated him into his own trade, which was that of tent-making, and thus Paul during his apostolic labors was able to defray the cost of his food and lodging by the work of his own hands (Acts 18:3; 1 Corinthians 4:12; 1 Thessalonians 2:9; 2 Thessalonians 3:8). Thirdly, in his father's house at Tarsus his education was strongly Pharisaic (Acts 23:6). To complete his schooling Paul was sent to Jerusalem, where he sat at the feet of the learned Gamaliel and was educated in the strict observance of the ancestral Law (Acts 22:3). Here he also acquired a good knowledge of exegesis and was trained in the practice of disputation. As a convinced and zealous Pharisee he returned to Tarsus before the public life of Christ opened in Palestine, for he never refers to personal acquaintance with Christ during the Savior's mortal life.

Some time after the death of our Lord Paul returned to Palestine. His profound conviction and emotional character made his zeal develop into a religious fanaticism against the infant Church. He took part in the stoning of the first martyr, St. Stephen, and in the fierce persecution of the Christians that followed.

Entrusted with a formal mission from the high priest, he departed for Damascus to arrest the Christians there and bring them bound to Jerusalem. As he was nearing Damascus, about noon, a light from heaven suddenly blazed round him. Jesus with His glorified body appeared to him and addressed him, turning him away from his apparently successful career. An immediate transformation was wrought in the soul of Paul. He was suddenly converted to the Christian faith and arose an Apostle (Acts 9:3–19; 22:6–16; 26:12–18).

He remained some days in Damascus after his Baptism (Acts 9:10–19), and then went to Arabia (Galatians 1:17), possibly for a year or two, to prepare himself for his future missionary activity. Having returned to Damascus, he stayed there for a time, preaching in the synagogues, that Jesus is the Christ, the Son of God. For this he incurred the hatred of the Jews and had to flee from the city (Acts 9:23–25; 2 Corinthians 11:32f). He then went to Jerusalem to see Peter (Galatians 1:18), to pay his homage to the head of the Church. Later he went back to his native Tarsus (Acts 9:30) and began to evangelize his own province (Galatians

1:21) until called by Barnabas to Antioch (Acts 11:25). After one year, on the occasion of a famine, both Barnabas and Paul were sent with alms to the poor Christian community at Jerusalem (Acts 11:27–30). Having fulfilled their mission, they returned to Antioch (Acts 12:5).

Soon after this Paul and Barnabas made the first missionary journey (A.D. 44/45–49/50), visiting the island of Cyprus, then Pamphylia, Pisidia, and Lycaonia, all in Asia Minor, and establishing churches at Pisidian Antioch, Iconium, Lystra, and Derbe (Acts 13–14).

After the Apostolic Council of Jerusalem, Paul, accompanied by Silas and later also by Timothy and Luke, made his second missionary journey (A.D. 50–52/53), first revisiting the churches previously established by him in Asia Minor and then passing through Galatia (Acts 16:6). At Troas a vision of a Macedonian was had by Paul, which impressed him as a call from God to evangelize Macedonia. He accordingly sailed for Europe and preached the Gospel in Philippi, Thessalonica, Beroea, Athens, and Corinth. Then he returned to Antioch by way of Ephesus and Jerusalem (Acts 15:36–18:22).

On his third missionary journey (A.D. 53/54–58) Paul visited nearly the same regions as on the second but made Ephesus, where he remained nearly three years, the center of his missionary activity. He laid plans also for another missionary journey, intending to leave Jerusalem for Rome and Spain. But persecutions by the Jews hindered him from accomplishing his purpose. After two years of imprisonment at Caesarea he finally reached Rome, where he was kept another two years in chains (Acts 18:23–28:31).

The Acts of the Apostles gives us no further information on the life of the Apostle. We gather, however, from the

Pastoral Epistles and from tradition that at the end of the two years St. Paul was released from his Roman imprisonment, and then travelled to Spain (Romans 15:24, 28), later to the East again, and then back to Rome, where he was imprisoned a second time, and in 67 was beheaded.

St. Paul's untiring interest in and paternal affection for the various churches established by him have given us 14 canonical Epistles. It is, however, quite certain that he wrote other letters which are no longer extant.

These Epistles are not arranged in our Bible according to chronological order. In the first place are given the Epistles addressed to communities, according to the relative dignity of the church receiving the Epistle, and the length of the subject matter; in the second place we have those addressed to individuals; and finally, the Epistle to the Hebrews.

All of the Epistles were written in Greek. Though St. Paul on occasion could speak that language with grace, he did not strive after literary elegance in his compositions. Because of the pressure of his work and cares, he usually dictated his Epistles and wrote the final salutation with his own hand (Romans 16:22; 1 Corinthians 16:21; Galatians 6:11; 2 Thessalonians 3:17). At times his thoughts are so overflowing and forceful that the rules of grammar and style are neglected. As a consequence, a mode of expression or an entire sentence is now and then difficult or obscure for us (2 Peter 3:16).

And yet, in spite of these grammatical faults and irregularities of style, no one can read the Epistles of St. Paul without being amazed at his natural eloquence. St. Jerome remarks that the words of the Apostle Paul seem to him like peals of thunder. His mental acumen and depth of feeling impart to his language loftiness, amazing power, and beauty.

A Note *about*
The Epistle of St. Paul the Apostle
to the Romans

St. Paul's Epistle to the Romans is given the position of honor at the head of all the New Testament Epistles. It was written at Corinth during the winter A.D. 57–58, at the close of St. Paul's third missionary journey, prior to his voyage to Jerusalem, where at the instigation of his bitter Jewish adversaries he was to be arrested and afterwards held prisoner for several years. This date for the composition of the Epistle is arrived at by comparing the circumstances and persons to which it alludes with those at Corinth during St. Paul's sojourn there at the close of his third missionary journey.

St. Paul during this period of his missionary activity had rather thoroughly covered the territory in the eastern world and was looking for new fields to evangelize in the West. He proposed, accordingly, after visiting Jerusalem, to journey to Spain, stopping en route at Rome. In this letter he wished to inform the Romans of his intended visit and to set before them the fruits of his meditations on the great religious question of the day, justification by faith and the relation of this new system of salvation to the Mosaic religion. Although he had previously dealt briefly with the question in the Epistle to the Galatians, St. Paul had not thus far had the opportunity of fully developing in writing his doctrine on this point. But now wishing to introduce himself to the Romans, he seized the opportunity of setting forth a lengthy statement and defense of his doctrine, not only for the Romans but also for the various Christian communities throughout the world.

The Epistle of St. Paul the Apostle
to the Romans

INTRODUCTION

Paul, the servant of Jesus Christ, called to be an apostle, set apart for the gospel of God, which he had promised beforehand through his prophets in the holy Scriptures, concerning his Son who was born to him according to the flesh of the offspring of David; who was foreordained Son of God by an act of power in keeping with the holiness of his spirit, by resurrection from the dead, Jesus Christ our Lord, through whom we have received the grace of apostleship to bring about obedience of faith among all the nations for his name's sake; among whom are you also called to be Jesus Christ's—to all God's beloved who are in Rome, called to be saints: grace be to you and peace from God our Father and from the Lord Jesus Christ.

First I give thanks to my God through Jesus Christ for all of you, because your faith is proclaimed all over the world. For God is my witness, whom I serve in my spirit in the gospel of his Son, how unceasingly I make mention of you, always imploring in my prayers that somehow I may at last by God's will come to you after a safe journey. For I long to see you that I may impart some spiritual grace unto you to strengthen you, that is, that among you I may be comforted together with you by that faith which is common to us both, yours and mine.

Now I would not, brethren, have you ignorant, that I have often intended to come to see you (and have been hindered until now) that I may produce some results among you also, as well as among the rest of the Gentiles. To Greeks and to foreigners, to learned and unlearned, I am debtor; so, for my part, I am ready to preach the gospel to you also who are at Rome.

For I am not ashamed of the gospel, for it is the power of God unto salvation to everyone who believes, to Jew first and then to Greek. For in it the justice of God is revealed, from faith unto faith, as it is written, "He who is just lives by faith."

I. DOCTRINAL
THE GOSPEL: THE POWER OF GOD FOR THE SALVATION OF ALL WHO BELIEVE

For the wrath of God is revealed from heaven against all ungodliness and wickedness of those men who in wickedness hold back the truth of God, seeing that what may be known about God is manifest to them. For God has manifested it to them. For since the creation of the world his invisible attributes are clearly seen—his everlasting power also and divinity—being understood through the things that are made. And so they are without excuse, seeing that,

8

although they knew God, they did not glorify him as God or give thanks, but became vain in their reasonings, and their senseless minds have been darkened. For while professing to be wise, they have become fools, and they have changed the glory of the incorruptible God for an image made like to corruptible man and to birds and four-footed beasts and creeping things.

Therefore God has given them up in the lustful desires of their hearts to uncleanness, so that they dishonor their own bodies among themselves—they who exchanged the truth of God for a lie, and worshipped and served the creature rather than the Creator who is blessed forever, amen.

For this cause God has given them up to shameful lusts; for their women have exchanged the natural use for that which is against nature, and in like manner the men also, having abandoned the natural use of the woman, have burned in their lusts one towards another, men with men doing shameless things and receiving in themselves the fitting recompense of their perversity. And as they have resolved against possessing the knowledge of God, God has given them up to a reprobate sense, so that they do what is not fitting; being filled with all iniquity, malice, immorality, avarice, wickedness; being full of envy, murder, contention, deceit, malignity; being whisperers, detractors, hateful to God, irreverent, proud, haughty, plotters of evil; disobedient to parents, foolish, dissolute, without affection, without fidelity, without mercy. Although they have known the ordinance of God, they have not understood that those who practice such things are deserving of death. And not only do they do these things, but they applaud others doing them.

Wherefore, thou art inexcusable, O man, whoever thou

art who judgest. For wherein thou judgest another, thou dost condemn thyself. For thou who judgest dost the same things thyself. And we know that the judgment of God is according to truth against those who do such things. But dost thou think, O man who judgest those who do such things and dost the same thyself, that thou wilt escape the judgment of God? Or dost thou despise the riches of his goodness and patience and long-suffering? Dost thou not know that the goodness of God is meant to lead thee to repentance? But according to thy hardness and unrepentant heart, thou dost treasure up to thyself wrath on the day of wrath and of the revelation of the just judgment of God, who will render to every man according to his works. Life eternal indeed he will give to those who by patience in good works seek glory and honor and immortality; but wrath and indignation to those who are contentious, and who do not submit to the truth but assent to iniquity. Tribulation and anguish shall be visited upon the soul of every man who works evil; of Jew first and then of Greek. But glory and honor and peace shall be awarded to everyone who does good, to Jew first and then to Greek. Because with God there is no respect of persons.

For whoever have sinned without the Law, will perish without the Law. For it is not they who hear the Law that are just in the sight of God; but it is they who follow the Law that will be justified. When the Gentiles who have no law do by nature what the Law prescribes, these having no law are a law unto themselves. They show the work of the Law written in their hearts. Their conscience bears witness to them, even when conflicting thoughts accuse or defend them. This will take place on the day when, according to my gospel, God will judge the hidden secrets of men through Jesus Christ.

But if thou art called "Jew," and dost rely upon the Law, and dost glory in God, and dost know his will, and dost approve the better things, being informed by the Law, thou art confident that thou art a guide to the blind, a light to those who walk in darkness, an instructor of the unwise, a teacher of children, having in the Law the pattern of knowledge and of truth. Thou therefore who teachest another, dost thou not teach thyself? Thou who preachest that men should not steal, dost thou steal? Thou who sayest that men should not commit adultery, dost thou commit adultery? Thou who dost abominate idols, dost thou commit sacrilege? Thou who dost glory in the Law, dost thou dishonor God by transgressing the Law? "For the name of God," as it is written, "is blasphemed through you among the Gentiles."

Circumcision, indeed, profits if thou keep the Law; but if thou be a transgressor of the Law, thy circumcision has become uncircumcision. Therefore if the uncircumcised keep the precepts of the Law, will not his uncircumcision be reckoned as circumcision? And he who is by nature uncircumcised, if he fulfill the Law, will judge thee who with the letter and circumcision art a transgressor of the Law. For he who is not a Jew who is so outwardly; nor is that circumcision which is so outwardly in the flesh; but he is a Jew who is so inwardly, and circumcision is a matter of the heart in the spirit, not in the letter. His praise is not from men but from God.

What advantage then remains to the Jew, or what is the use of circumcision? Much in every respect. First, indeed, because the oracles of God were entrusted to them. For what if some of them have not believed? Will their unbelief make void the fidelity of God? By no means! For God is true, and every man is a liar, as it is written, "That thou mayest be justified in thy words, and mayest be victorious when thou art judged." But if our wickedness show forth the justice of God, what shall we say? Is God unjust who inflicts punishment? (I speak after a purely human manner.) By no means! Otherwise, how is God to judge the world? But if through my lie the truth of God has abounded unto his glory, why am I also still judged a sinner? And why should we not, as some calumniously accuse us of teaching, do evil that good may come from it? The condemnation of such is just.

What then? Are we better off than they? Not at all. For we have argued that Jews and Greeks are all under sin, as it is written, "There is not one just man; there is none who understands; there is none who seeks after God. All have gone astray together; they have become worthless. There is none who does good, no, not even one. Their throat is an open sepulchre; with their tongues they have dealt deceitfully. The venom of asps is beneath their lips; their mouth is full of cursing and bitterness. Their feet are swift to shed blood; destruction and misery are in their ways. And the path of peace they have not known. There is no fear of God before their eyes."

Now we know that whatever the Law says, it is speaking to those who are under the Law; in order that every mouth may be shut, and the whole world may be made subject to God. For by the works of the Law no human being shall be justified before him, for through law comes the recognition of sin.

But now the justice of God has been made manifest

independently of the Law, being attested by the Law and the Prophets; the justice of God through faith in Jesus Christ upon all who believe. For there is no distinction, as all have sinned and have need of the glory of God. They are justified freely by his grace through the redemption which is in Christ Jesus, whom God has set forth as a propitiation by his blood through faith, to manifest his justice, God in his patience remitting former sins; to manifest his justice at the present time, so that he himself is just, and makes just him who has faith in Jesus.

Where then is thy boasting? It is excluded. By what law? Of works? No, but by the law of faith. For we reckon that a man is justified by faith independently of the works of the Law. Is God the God of the Jews only, and not of the Gentiles also? For there is but one God who will justify the circumcised by faith, and the uncircumcised through the same faith. Do we therefore through faith destroy the Law? By no means! Rather we establish the Law.

What then shall we say that Abraham, our father according to the flesh, acquired? For if Abraham was justified by works, he has reason to boast, but not before God. For what does the Scripture say? "Abraham believed God and it was credited to him as justice." Now to him who works, the reward is not credited as a favor but as something due. But to him who does not work, but believes in him who justifies the impious, his faith is credited to him as justice. Thus David declares the blessedness of the man to whom God credits justice without works: "Blessed are they whose iniquities are forgiven, and whose sins are covered; blessed is the man to whom the Lord will not credit sin."

Does this blessedness hold good, then, only for the

circumcised, or also for the uncircumcised? For we say that unto Abraham faith was credited as justice. How then was it credited? When he was in the state of circumcision or in that of uncircumcision? Not in circumcision but in uncircumcision. And he received the sign of circumcision as the seal of the justice of faith which he had while uncircumcised, in order that he may be the father of all who, while uncircumcised, believed, that to them also it may be credited as justice; and the father of the circumcised, not of those merely who are circumcised, but also of those who follow in the steps of the faith that was our father Abraham's while yet uncircumcised.

For not through the Law but through the justice of faith was the promise made to Abraham and to his posterity that he should be heir of the world. For if they who are of the Law are heirs, faith is made empty, the promise is made void. For the Law works wrath; for where there is no law, neither is there transgression. Therefore the promise was the outcome of faith, that it might be a favor, in order that it might be secure for all the offspring, not only for those who are of the Law, but also for those who are of the faith of Abraham, who is the father of us all; as it is written, "I have appointed thee the father of many nations." He is our father in the sight of God, whom he believed, who gives life to the dead and calls things that are not as though they were.

Abraham hoping against hope believed, so that he became the father of many nations, according to what was said, "So shall thy offspring be." And without weakening in faith, he considered his own deadened body (for he was almost a hundred years old) and the deadened womb of Sara; and yet in view of the promise of God, he did not waver through unbelief but was strengthened in faith, giving glory to God, being fully aware that whatever God has promised he is able also to perform. Therefore it was credited to him as justice.

Now not for his sake only was it written that "It was credited to him," but for the sake of us also, to whom it will be credited if we believe in him who raised Jesus our Lord from the dead, who was delivered up for our sins, and rose again for our justification.

Having been justified therefore by faith, let us have peace with God through our Lord Jesus Christ, through whom we also have access by faith unto that grace in which we stand, and exult in the hope of the glory of the sons of God. And not only this, but we exult in tribulation also, knowing that tribulation works out endurance, and endurance tried virtue, and tried virtue hope. And hope does not disappoint, because the charity of God is poured forth in our hearts by the Holy Spirit who has been given to us. For why did Christ, at the set time, die for the wicked when as yet we were weak? For scarcely on behalf of a just man does one die; yet perhaps one might bring himself to die for a good man. But God commends his charity towards us, because when as yet we were sinners, Christ died for us.

Much more now that we are justified by his blood, shall we be saved through him from the wrath. For if when we were enemies we were reconciled to God by the death of his Son, much more, having been reconciled, shall we be saved by his life. And not this only, but we exult also in God through our Lord Jesus Christ, through whom we have now received reconciliation.

Therefore as through one man sin entered into the world

and through sin death, and thus death has passed unto all men because all have sinned—for until the Law sin was in the world, but sin is not imputed when there is no law; yet death reigned from Adam until Moses even over those who did not sin after the likeness of the transgression of Adam, who is a figure of him who was to come.

But not like the offense is the gift. For if by the offense of the one the many died, much more has the grace of God, and the gift in the grace of the one man Jesus Christ, abounded unto the many. Nor is the gift as it was in the case of one man's sin, for the judgment was from one man unto condemnation, but grace is from many offenses unto justification. For if by reason of the one man's offense death reigned through the one man, much more will they who receive the abundance of the grace and of the gift of justice reign in life through the one Jesus Christ. Therefore as from the offense of the one man the result was unto condemnation to all men, so from the justice of the one the result is unto justification of life to all men. For just as by the disobedience of the one man the many were constituted sinners, so also by the obedience of the one the many will be constituted just.

Now the Law intervened that the offense might abound. But where the offense has abounded, grace has abounded yet more; so that as sin has reigned unto death, so also grace may reign by justice unto life everlasting through Jesus Christ our Lord.

What then shall we say? Shall we continue in sin that grace may abound? By no means! For how shall we who are dead to sin still live in it? Do you not know that all we who have been baptized into Christ Jesus have been baptized into his death? For we were buried with him by means of Baptism into death, in order that, just as Christ has arisen from the dead through the glory of the Father, so we also may walk in newness of life. For if we have been united with him in the likeness of his death, we shall be so in the likeness of his resurrection also. For we know that our old self has been crucified with him, in order that the body of sin may be destroyed, that we may no longer be slaves to sin; for he who is dead is acquitted of sin. But if we have died with Christ, we believe that we shall also live together with Christ; for we know that Christ, having risen from the dead, dies now no more, death shall no longer have dominion over him. For the death that he died, he died to sin once for all, but the life that he lives, he lives unto God. Thus do you consider yourselves also as dead to sin, but alive to God in Christ Jesus.

Therefore do not let sin reign in your mortal body so that you obey its lusts. And do not yield your members to sin as weapons of iniquity, but present yourselves to God as those who have come to life from the dead and your members as weapons of justice for God; for sin shall not have dominion over you, since you are not under the Law but under grace.

What then? Are we to sin because we are not under the Law but under grace? By no means! Do you not know that to whom you offer yourselves as slaves for obedience, to him whom you obey you are the slaves, whether to sin unto death or to obedience unto justice? But thanks be to God that you who were the slaves of sin have now been delivered, and having been set free from sin, you have become the slaves of justice. I speak in a human way because of the weakness of your flesh; for as you yielded your members as slaves of uncleanness and iniquity unto iniquity, so now yield your members as slaves of justice unto sanctification.

For when you were the slaves of sin, you were free as regards justice. But what fruit had you then from those things of which you are now ashamed? For the end of these things is death. But now set free from sin and become slaves to God, you have your fruit unto sanctification, and as your end, life everlasting. For the wages of sin is death, but the gift of God is life everlasting in Christ Jesus our Lord.

Do you not know, brethren (for I speak to those who know law), that the Law has dominion over a man as long as he lives? For the married woman is bound by the Law while her husband is alive; but if her husband die, she is set free from the law of the husband. Therefore while her husband is alive, she will be called an adulteress if she be with another man; but if her husband dies, she is set free from the law of the husband, so that she is not an adulteress if she has been with another man. Therefore, my brethren, you also, through the body of Christ, have been made to die to the Law, so as to belong to another who has risen from the dead, in order that we may bring forth fruit unto God. For when we were in the flesh the sinful passions, which were aroused by the Law, were at work in our members so that they brought forth fruit unto death. But now we have been set free from the Law, having died to that by which we were held down, so that we may serve in a new spirit and not according to the outworn letter.

What shall we say then? Is the Law sin? By no means! Yet I did not know sin save through the Law. For I had not known lust unless the Law had said, "Thou shalt not lust." But sin, having found an occasion, worked in me by means of the commandment all manner of lust, for without the Law sin was dead. Once upon a time I was living without law, but when the commandment came, sin revived, and I died, and the commandment that was unto life was discovered in my case to be unto death. For sin, having taken occasion from the commandment, deceived me, and through it killed me. So that the Law indeed is holy and the commandment holy and just and good.

Did then that which is good become death to me? By no means! But sin, that it might be manifest as sin, worked death for me through that which is good, in order that sin by reason of the commandment might become immeasurably sinful. For we know that the Law is spiritual but I am carnal, sold into the power of sin. For I do not understand what I do, for it is not what I wish that I do, but what I hate, that I do. But if I do what I do not wish, I admit that the Law is good. Now therefore it is no longer I who do it, but the sin that dwells in me. For I know that in me, that is, in my flesh, no good dwells, because to wish is within my power, but I do not find the strength to accomplish what is good. For I do not the good that I wish, but the evil that I do not wish, that I perform. Now if I do what I do not wish, it is no longer I who do it, but the sin that dwells in me. Therefore, when I wish to do good I discover this law, namely, that evil is at hand for me. For I am delighted with the law of God according to the inner man, but I see another law in my members, warring against the law of my mind and making me prisoner to the law of sin that is in my members.

Unhappy man that I am! Who will deliver me from the body of this death? The grace of God through Jesus Christ our Lord. Therefore I myself with my mind serve the law of God, but with my flesh the law of sin.

There is therefore now no condemnation for those who

are in Christ Jesus, who do not walk according to the flesh. For the law of the Spirit of the life in Christ Jesus has delivered me from the law of sin and of death. For what was impossible to the Law, in that it was weak because of the flesh, God has made good. By sending his Son in the likeness of sinful flesh as a sin-offering, in order that the requirements of the Law might be fulfilled in us, who walk not according to the flesh but according to the spirit.

Now they who are according to the flesh mind the things of the flesh, but they who are according to the spirit mind the things of the spirit. For the inclination of the flesh is death, but the inclination of the spirit, life and peace. For the wisdom of the flesh is hostile to God, for it is not subject to the law of God, nor can it be. And they who are carnal cannot please God.

You, however, are not carnal but spiritual, if indeed the Spirit of God dwells in you. But if anyone does not have the Spirit of Christ, he does not belong to Christ. But if Christ is in you, the body, it is true, is dead by reason of sin, but the spirit is life by reason of justification. But if the Spirit of him who raised Jesus from the dead dwells in you, then he who raised Jesus Christ from the dead will also bring to life your mortal bodies because of his Spirit who dwells in you.

Therefore, brethren, we are debtors, not to the flesh, that we should live according to the flesh, for if you live according to the flesh you will die; but if by the spirit you put to death the deeds of the flesh, you will live.

For whoever are led by the Spirit of God, they are the sons of God. Now you have not received a spirit of bondage so as to be again in fear, but you have received a spirit of adoption as sons, by virtue of which we cry, "Abba! Father!"

The Spirit himself gives testimony to our spirit that we are sons of God. But if we are sons, we are heirs also: heirs indeed of God and joint heirs with Christ, provided, however, we suffer with him that we may also be glorified with him.

For I reckon that the sufferings of the present time are not worthy to be compared with the glory to come that will be revealed in us. For the eager longing of creation awaits the revelation of the sons of God. For creation was made subject to vanity—not by its own will but by reason of him who made it subject—in hope, because creation itself also will be delivered from its slavery to corruption into the freedom of the glory of the sons of God. For we know that all creation groans and travails in pain until now.

And not only it, but we ourselves also who have the firstfruits of the Spirit—we ourselves groan within ourselves, waiting for the adoption as sons, the redemption of our body. For in hope were we saved. But hope that is seen is not hope. For how can a man hope for what he sees? But if we hope for what we do not see, we wait for it with patience.

But in like manner the Spirit also helps our weakness. For we do not know what we should pray for as we ought, but the Spirit himself pleads for us with unutterable groanings. And he who searches the hearts knows what the Spirit desires, that he pleads for the saints according to God.

Now we know that for those who love God all things work together unto good, for those who, according to his purpose, are saints through his call. For those whom he has foreknown he has also predestined to become conformed to the image of his Son, that he should be the firstborn among many brethren. And those whom he has predestined, them he has also called; and those whom he has called, them he has also justified, and those whom he has justified, them he has also glorified.

What then shall we say to these things? If God is for us, who is against us? He who has not spared even his own Son but has delivered him for us all, how can he fail to grant us also all things with him? Who shall make accusation against the elect of God? It is God who justifies! Who shall condemn? It is Christ Jesus who died; yes, and rose again, he who is at the right hand of God, who also intercedes for us!

Who shall separate us from the love of Christ? Shall tribulation, or distress, or persecution, or hunger, or nakedness, or danger, or the sword? Even as it is written, "For thy sake we are put to death all the day long. We are regarded as sheep for the slaughter." But in all these things we overcome because of him who has loved us. For I am sure that neither death, nor life, nor angels, nor principalities, nor things present, nor things to come, nor powers, nor height, nor depth, nor any other creature will be able to separate us from the love of God, which is in Christ Jesus our Lord.

I speak the truth in Christ, I do not lie, my conscience bearing me witness in the Holy Spirit, that I have great sadness and continuous sorrow in my heart. For I could wish to be anathema myself from Christ for the sake of my brethren, who are my kinsmen according to the flesh; who are Israelites, who have the adoption as sons, and the glory and the covenants and the legislation and the worship and the promises; who have the fathers, and from whom is the Christ according to the flesh, who is, over all things, God blessed forever, amen.

It is not that the word of God has failed. For they are not all Israelites who are sprung from Israel; nor because they are the descendants of Abraham, are they all his children; but "Through Isaac shall thy posterity bear thy name." That is to say, they are not sons of God who are the children of the flesh, but it is the children of promise who are reckoned as posterity. For this is a word of promise: "About this time I will come and Sara shall have a son." And not she only but also Rebecca, who conceived by one man, Isaac our father; for before the children had yet been born, or had done aught of good or evil, in order that the selective purpose of God might stand, depending not on deeds, but on him who calls, it was said to her, "The elder shall serve the younger"; as it is written, "Jacob I have loved, but Esau I have hated."

What then shall we say? Is there injustice with God? By no means! For he says to Moses, "I will have mercy on whom I have mercy, and I will show pity to whom I will show pity." So then there is question not of him who wills nor of him who runs, but of God showing mercy. For Scripture says to Pharaoh, "For this very purpose I have raised thee up that I may show in thee my power, and that my name may be proclaimed in all the earth." Therefore he has mercy on whom he will, and whom he will he hardens.

Thou sayest to me: Why then does he still find fault? For who resists his will? O man, who art thou to reply to God? Does the object moulded say to him who moulded it: Why hast thou made me thus? Or is not the potter master of his clay, to make from the same mass one vessel for honorable, another for ignoble use? But what if God, wishing to show his wrath and to make known his power, endured with much patience vessels of wrath, ready for destruction, that he might show the riches of his glory upon vessels of mercy, which he has prepared unto glory—even us whom he has called not only from among the Jews but also from among the Gentiles?

As he says in Osee, "A people not mine I will call my people, and an unbeloved, beloved, and her who had not obtained mercy, one who has obtained mercy. And it shall be in the place where it was said to them: you are not my people; there they shall be called sons of the living God." And Isaias cries out concerning Israel, "Though the number of the children of Israel are as the sands of the sea, the remnant shall be saved. For the Lord fulfills his word speedily in justice, because a speedy word will the Lord accomplish on earth." And as Isaias foretold, "Unless the Lord of Hosts had left us a posterity, we should have become as Sodom and should have been like Gomorrah."

What then shall we say? That the Gentiles who were not pursuing justice have secured justice, but a justice that is from faith; but Israel, by pursuing a law of justice, has not attained to the law of justice. And why? Because they sought it not from faith, but as it were from works. For they stumbled at the stumbling-stone, as it is written, "Behold I lay in Sion a stumbling-stone and rock of scandal: and whoever believes in him shall not be disappointed."

Brethren, my heart's desire and my prayer to God is in their behalf unto their salvation. For I bear them witness that they have zeal for God, but not according to knowledge; for, ignorant of the justice of God and seeking to establish their own, they have not submitted to the justice of God. For Christ is the consummation of the Law unto justice for everyone who believes.

For Moses wrote that the man who does that justice which is of the Law shall live by it. But the justice that is of faith says, "Do not say in thy heart: Who shall ascend into heaven?" (that is, to bring down Christ); "or, Who shall descend into the abyss?" (that is, to bring up Christ from the dead). But what does it say? "The word is near thee, in thy mouth and in thy heart" (that is, the word of faith, which we preach). For if thou confess with thy mouth that Jesus is the Lord, and believe in thy heart that God has raised him from the dead, thou shalt be saved. For with the heart a man believes unto justice, and with the mouth profession of faith is made unto salvation. For the Scripture says, "Whoever believes in him shall not be disappointed." For there is no distinction between Jew and Greek, for there is the same Lord of all, rich towards all who call upon him. "For whoever calls upon the name of the Lord shall be saved."

How then are they to call upon him in whom they have not believed? But how are they to believe him whom they have not heard? And how are they to hear, if no one preaches? And how are men to preach unless they be sent? As it is written, "How beautiful are the feet of those who preach the gospel of peace; of those who bring glad tidings of good things!" But all did not obey the gospel. For Isaias says, "Lord, who has believed our report?" Faith then depends on hearing, and hearing on the word of Christ. But I say: Have they not heard? Yes, indeed, "Their voice has gone forth into all the earth, and their words unto the ends of the world." But I say: Has not Israel known? First of all, Moses says, "I will provoke you to jealousy of those who are not a nation; I will stir you to anger against a senseless nation." Then Isaias dares to say, "I was found by those who did not seek me; I appeared openly to those who made no inquiry of me." But to Israel he says, "All the day long I stretched out my hand to a people unbelieving and contradicting."

I say then: Has God cast off his people? By no means! For I also am an Israelite of the posterity of Abraham, of the tribe of Benjamin. God has not cast off his people whom he foreknew. Or do you not know what the Scripture says in the account of Elias, how he lodges complaint with God against Israel? "Lord, they have slain thy prophets, they have razed thy altars; and I only am left, and they are seeking my life." But what does the divine answer say to him? "I have left for myself seven thousand men, who have not bowed their knees to Baal." Even so, then, at the present time there is a remnant left, selected out of grace. And if out of grace, then not in virtue of works; otherwise grace is no longer grace.

What then? What Israel was seeking after, that it has not obtained; but the chosen have obtained it, and the rest have been blinded, as it is written, "God has given them a spirit of stupor until this present day, eyes that they may not see, and ears that they may not hear." And David says, "Let their table become a snare and a trap and a stumbling-block and a recompense unto them; let their eyes be darkened that they may not see, and let them bow their backs always."

I say then: have they so stumbled as to fall? By no means! But by their offense salvation has come to the Gentiles, that they may be jealous of them. Now if their offense is the riches of the world, and their decline the riches of the Gentiles, how much more their full number!

For I say to you Gentiles: As long, indeed, as I am an apostle of the Gentiles, I will honor my ministry, in the hope that I may provoke to jealousy those who are my flesh, and may save some of them. For if the rejection of them is the reconciliation of the world, what will the reception of them be but life from the dead? Now if the first handful of the dough is holy, so also is the lump of dough; and if the root is holy, so also are the branches. But if some of the branches have been broken off, and if thou, being a wild olive, art grafted in their place, and hast become a partaker of the stem and fatness of the olive tree, do not boast against the branches. But if thou dost boast, still it is not thou that supportest the stem, but the stem thee. Thou wilt say, then, "Branches were broken off that I might be grafted in." True, but they were broken off because of unbelief, whereas thou by faith standest. Be not high-minded, but fear. For if God has not spared the natural branches, perhaps he may not spare thee either. See, then, the goodness and severity of God: his severity towards those who have fallen, but the goodness of God towards thee if thou abides in his goodness; otherwise thou also wilt be cut off.

And they also, if they do not continue in unbelief, will be grafted in; for God is able to graft them back. For if thou hast been cut off from the wild olive tree which is natural to thee, and contrary to nature, hast been grafted into the cultivated olive tree, how much more shall these, the natural branches, be grafted into their own olive tree!

For I would not, brethren, have you ignorant of this mystery, lest you should be wise in your own conceits, that a partial blindness only has befallen Israel, until the full number of the Gentiles should enter, and thus all Israel shall be saved, as it is written, "There will come out of Sion the deliverer and he will turn away impiety from Jacob; and this is my covenant with them, when I shall take away their sins." In view of the gospel, they are enemies for your sake; but in view of the divine choice, they are most dear for the sake of the fathers. For the gifts and the call of God are without repentance.

For as you also at one time did not believe God, but now have obtained mercy by reason of their unbelief, so they too have not now believed by reason of the mercy shown you, that they too may obtain mercy. For God has shut up all in unbelief, that he may have mercy upon all.

Oh, the depth of the riches of the wisdom and of the knowledge of God! How incomprehensible are his judgments and how unsearchable his ways! For "Who has known the mind of the Lord, or who has been his counsellor? Or who has first given to him, that recompense should be made him?" For from him and through him and unto him are all things. To him be the glory forever, amen.

II. MORAL

I exhort you therefore, brethren, by the mercy of God, to present your bodies as a sacrifice, living, holy, pleasing to God—your spiritual service. And be not conformed to this world, but be transformed in the newness of your mind, that you may discern what is the good and acceptable and perfect will of God.

By the grace that has been given to me, I say to each one among you: let no one rate himself more than he ought, but let him rate himself according to moderation, and according as God has apportioned to each one the measure of faith. For just as in one body we have many members, yet all the members have not the same function, so we, the many, are one body in Christ, but severally members one of another. But we have gifts differing according to the grace that has been given us, such as prophecy to be used according to the proportion of faith; or ministry, in ministering; or he who teaches, in teaching; he who exhorts, in exhorting; he who gives, in simplicity; he who presides, with carefulness; he who shows mercy, with cheerfulness.

Let love be without pretense. Hate what is evil, hold to what is good. Love one another with fraternal charity, anticipating one another with honor. Be not slothful in zeal; be fervent in spirit, serving the Lord, rejoicing in hope. Be patient in tribulation, persevering in prayer. Share the needs of the saints, practising hospitality. Bless those who persecute you; bless and do not curse. Rejoice with those who rejoice; weep with those who weep. Be of one mind towards one another. Do not set your mind on high things but condescend to the lowly. Be not wise in your own conceits. To no man render evil for evil, but provide good things not only in the sight of God, but also in the sight of all men. If it be possible, as far as in you lies, be at peace with all men. Do not avenge yourselves, beloved, but give place to the wrath, for it is written, "Vengeance is mine; I will repay, says the Lord." But "If thy enemy is hungry, give him food; if he is thirsty, give him drink; for by so doing thou wilt heap coals of fire upon his head." Be not overcome by evil, but overcome evil with good.

Let everyone be subject to the higher authorities, for there exists no authority except from God, and those who exist have been appointed by God. Therefore he who resists the authority resists the ordinance of God; and they that resist bring on themselves condemnation. For rulers are a terror not to the good work but to the evil. Dost thou wish, then, not to fear the authority? Do what is good and thou wilt have praise from it. For it is God's minister to thee for good. But if thou dost what is evil, fear, for not without reason does it carry the sword. For it is God's minister, an avenger to execute wrath on him who does evil. Wherefore you must needs be subject, not only because of the wrath, but also for conscience' sake. For this is also why you pay tribute, for they are the ministers of God, serving unto this very end. Render to all men whatever is their due; tribute to whom tribute is due; taxes to whom taxes are due; fear to whom fear is due; honor to whom honor is due.

Owe no man anything except to love one another; for he who loves his neighbor has fulfilled the Law. For "Thou shalt not commit adultery; Thou shalt not kill; Thou shalt not steal; Thou shalt not covet"; and if there is any other commandment, it is summed up in this saying, "Thou shalt love thy neighbor as thyself." Love does no evil to a neighbor. Love therefore is the fulfillment of the Law.

And this do, understanding the time, for it is now the hour for us to rise from sleep, because now our salvation is nearer than when we came to believe. The night is far advanced; the day is at hand. Let us therefore lay aside the works of darkness, and put on the armor of light. Let us walk becomingly as in the day, not in revelry and drunkenness, not in debauchery and wantonness, not in strife and jealousy. But put on the Lord Jesus Christ, and as for the flesh, take no thought for its lusts.

But him who is weak in faith, receive without disputes about opinions. For one believes that he may eat all things; but he who is weak, let him eat vegetables. Let not him who eats despise him who does not eat, and let not him who does not eat judge him who eats; for God has received him. Who art thou to judge another's servant? To his own lord he stands or falls; but he will stand, for God is able to make him stand. For one esteems one day above another; another esteems every day alike. Let everyone be convinced in his own mind. He who regards the day, regards it for the Lord; and he who eats, eats for the Lord, for he gives thanks to God. And he who does not eat, abstains for the Lord, and gives thanks to God. For none of us lives to himself, and none dies to himself; for if we live, we live to the Lord, or if we die, we die to the Lord. Therefore, whether we live or die, we are the Lord's. For to this end Christ died and rose again, that he might be Lord both of the dead and of the living. But thou, why dost thou judge thy brother? Or thou, why dost thou despise thy brother? For we shall all stand at the judgment-seat of God; for it is written, "As I live, says the Lord, to me every knee shall bend, and every tongue shall give praise to God."

Therefore every one of us will render an account for himself to God. Therefore let us no longer judge one another, but rather judge this, that you should not put a stumbling-block or a hindrance in your brother's way. I know and am confident in the Lord Jesus that nothing is of itself unclean; but to him who regards anything as unclean, to him it is unclean. If, then, thy brother is grieved because of thy food, no longer dost thou walk according to charity. Do not with thy food destroy him for whom Christ died. Let not, then, our good be reviled. For the kingdom of God does not consist in food and drink, but in justice and peace and joy in the Holy Spirit; for he who in this way serves Christ pleases God and is approved by men. Let us, then, follow after the things that make for peace, and let us safeguard the things that make for mutual edification. Do not for the sake of food destroy the work of God! All things indeed are clean; but a thing is evil for the man who eats through scandal. It is good not to eat meat and not to drink wine, nor to do anything by which thy brother is offended or scandalized or weakened. Thou hast faith. Keep it to thyself before God. Blessed is he who does not condemn himself by what he approves. But he who hesitates, if he eats, is condemned, because it is not from faith; for all that is not from faith is sin.

Now we, the strong, ought to bear the infirmities of the weak, and not to please ourselves. Let every one of you please his neighbor by doing good, for his edification; for Christ did not please himself, but as it is written, "The reproaches of those who reproach thee have fallen upon me." For whatever things have been written have been written for our instruction, that through the patience and the consolation afforded by the Scriptures we may have hope. May then the God of patience and of comfort grant you to be of one mind towards one another according to Jesus Christ; that, one in spirit, you may with one mouth glorify the God and Father of our Lord Jesus Christ.

Wherefore receive one another, even as Christ has received you to the honor of God. For I say that Christ Jesus has been a minister of the circumcision in order to show God's fidelity in confirming the promises made to our fathers, but that the Gentiles glorify God because of his mercy, as it is written, "Therefore will I praise thee among the Gentiles, and will sing to thy name." And again he says, "Rejoice, you Gentiles, with his people." And again, "Praise the Lord, all you Gentiles; and sing his praises, all you peoples." And again Isaias says, "There shall be the root of Jesse, and he who shall arise to rule the Gentiles . . . in him the Gentiles shall hope." Now may the God of hope fill you with all joy and peace in believing, that you may abound in hope and in the power of the Holy Spirit.

CONCLUSION

Now I for my part, my brethren, am convinced with regard to you that you yourselves are full of love, filled with all knowledge, so that you are able to admonish one another. But I have written to you rather boldly here and there, brethren—as it were to refresh your memory—because of the grace that has been given me by God, that I should be a minister of Christ Jesus to the Gentiles; sanctifying the gospel of God, that the offering up of the Gentiles may become acceptable, being sanctified by the Holy Spirit. I have therefore this boast in Christ Jesus as regards the work of God. For I do not make bold to mention anything but what Christ has wrought through me to bring about the obedience of the Gentiles, by word and deed, with mighty signs and wonders, by the power of the Holy Spirit, so that from Jerusalem round about as far as Illyricum I have completed the evangelization of Christ. But I have not preached this gospel where Christ has already been named, lest I might build on another man's foundation; but even as it is written, "They who have not been told of him shall see, and they who have not heard shall understand."

This is why I was hindered these many times from coming

to you. But now, having no more work in these parts, and having had for many years a great desire to come to you, when I set out for Spain I hope to see you as I pass through (and by you to be sped on my way there), having first enjoyed being with you for a while. Now, however, I will set out for Jerusalem to minister to the saints. For Macedonia and Achaia have thought it well to make a contribution for the poor among the saints at Jerusalem. So it has pleased them, and their debtors they are. For if the Gentiles have shared in their spiritual blessings, they should also minister to them in material things. Therefore, when I have completed this, and have delivered to them the proceeds, I will set out by way of you for Spain. And I know that when I come to you, I shall come with the fullness of Christ's blessing.

Now I exhort you, brethren, through our Lord Jesus Christ, and through the charity of the Spirit, that you help me by your prayers to God for me, that I may be delivered from the unbelievers in Judea, and that the offering of my service may be acceptable to the saints in Jerusalem; that I may come to you in joy, by the will of God, and may be refreshed with you. Now the God of peace be with you all. Amen.

But I commend to you Phoebe, our sister, who is in the ministry of the church at Cenchrae, that you may receive her in the Lord as becomes saints, and that you may assist her in whatever business she may have need of you. For she too has assisted many, including myself.

Greet Prisca and Aquila, my helpers in Christ Jesus, who for my life have risked their own necks. To them not only I give thanks but also all the churches of the Gentiles. Greet also the church that is in their house. Greet my beloved

Epaenetus, who is the first-fruits of Asia to Christ. Greet Mary who has labored much among you. Greet Andronicus and Junias, my kinsmen and my fellow-prisoners, who are distinguished among the apostles, who also were in Christ before me. Greet Ampliatus, beloved to me in the Lord. Greet Urbanus, our helper in Christ, and my beloved Stachys. Greet Apelles, approved in Christ. Greet the members of Aristobulus' household. Greet Herodion, my kinsman. Greet the members of Narcissus' household who are in the Lord. Greet Tryphaena and Tryphosa who labor in the Lord. Greet the beloved Persis who has labored much in the Lord. Greet Rufus, the elect in the Lord, and her who is his mother and mine. Greet Asyncritus, Phlegon, Hermas, Patrobas, Hermes, and the brethren was are with them. Greet Philologus and Julia, Nereus and his sister, and Olympias, and all the saints who are with them. Greet one another with a holy kiss. All the churches of Christ greet you.

Now I exhort you, brethren, that you watch those who cause dissensions and scandals contrary to the doctrine that you have learned, and avoid them. For such do not serve Christ our Lord but their own belly, and by smooth words and flattery deceive the hearts of the simple. For your submission to the faith has been published everywhere. I rejoice therefore over you. Yet I would have you wise as to what is good, and guileless as to what is evil. But the God of peace will speedily crush Satan under your feet. The grace of our Lord Jesus Christ be with you.

Timothy, my fellow-laborer, greets you, and Lucius, and Jason, and Sosipater, my kinsmen. I, Tertius, who have written this epistle, greet you in the Lord. Gaius, my host, and the host of the whole church, greets you. Erastus, the city treasurer, and Quartus, our brother, greet you. [May the grace of our Lord Jesus Christ be with you all, amen.]

Now to him who is able to strengthen you in accordance with my gospel, and the preaching of Jesus Christ, according to the revelation of the mystery which has been kept in silence from eternal ages, which is manifest now through the writings of the prophets according to the precept of the eternal God, and made known to all the Gentiles to bring about obedience to faith—to the only wise God, through Jesus Christ, be honor forever and ever. Amen.

A Note *about*
The First Epistle of St. Paul the Apostle
to the Corinthians

Corinth was a Roman colony built upon the remains of an old Greek city. At the time of the Apostles it was materially prosperous and morally corrupt.

On his second missionary journey, Paul preached about two years in Corinth, first to the Jews in the synagogue and then to the Gentiles in the house of Titus Justus (Acts 18:1–18). After his disappointment in the use of a philosophical approach to Christianity at Athens (Acts 17:15ff), Paul used at Corinth a simpler presentation of his doctrine. According to the divine promise (Acts 18:9f), he made many converts but suffered much from the hostility of the Jews. He left for Ephesus some time after Gallio became proconsul of Achaia, i.e., about A.D. 52.

It is quite probable that St. Paul wrote an Epistle to the Corinthians prior to the two that we now possess (1 Corinthians 5:9). The Epistle called St. Paul's First to the Corinthians was occasioned by the visit to Ephesus of members of the Corinthian church (1 Corinthians 1:11; 16:12, 17). St. Paul, who had meanwhile returned to Antioch and undertaken his third missionary journey, learned from these messengers of certain disorders in the church at Corinth. Questions were also proposed by the neophytes to their spiritual father for solution. To correct those disorders and to answer these questions, St. Paul wrote this masterly Epistle.

From 1 Corinthians 16:5–8 it is clear that the letter was written at Ephesus some time before Pentecost, probably in the beginning of the year A.D. 57.

The First Epistle of St. Paul the Apostle
to the Corinthians

INTRODUCTION

Paul, called by the will of God to be an apostle of Jesus
Christ, and Sosthenes our brother, to the church of God
at Corinth, to you who have been sanctified in Christ Jesus
and called to be saints with all who call upon the name of
our Lord Jesus Christ in every place—their Lord as well as
ours. Grace be to you and peace from God our Father and
the Lord Jesus Christ.

I give thanks to my God always concerning you for the
grace of God which was given you in Christ Jesus, because
in everything you have been enriched in him, in all utterance and in all knowledge; even as the witness to the Christ
has been made so firm in you that you lack no grace, while
awaiting the appearance of our Lord Jesus Christ, who will
also keep you secure unto the end, unimpeachable in the day
of the coming of our Lord Jesus Christ. God is trustworthy,
by him you have been called into fellowship with his Son,
Jesus Christ our Lord.

I. PARTY SPIRIT

Now I beseech you, brethren, by the name of our Lord Jesus
Christ, that you all say the same thing; and that there be no
dissensions among you, but that you be perfectly united in
one mind and in one judgment. For I have been informed
about you, my brethren, by those of the house of Chloe,
that there are strifes among you. Now this is what I mean:
each of you says, I am of Paul, or I am of Apollos, or I am of
Cephas, or I am of Christ. Has Christ been divided up? Was
Paul crucified for you? Or were you baptized in the name of
Paul? I thank God that I baptized none of you but Crispus
and Gaius, lest anyone should say that you were baptized
in my name. I baptized also the household of Stephanas, I
am not aware of having baptized anyone else.

For Christ did not send me to baptize, but to preach the
gospel, not with wisdom of words, lest the cross of Christ
be made void. For the doctrine of the cross is foolishness
to those who perish, but to those who are saved, that is, to
us, it is the power of God. For it is written, "I will destroy
the wisdom of the wise, and the prudence of the prudent I
will reject." Where is the "wise man"? Where is the scribe?
Where is the disputant of this world? Has not God turned to
foolishness the "wisdom" of this world? For since, in God's
wisdom, the world did not come to know God by "wisdom,"
it pleased God, by the foolishness of our preaching, to save
those who believe. For the Jews ask for signs, and the Greeks
look for "wisdom"; but we, for our part, preach a crucified
Christ—to the Jews indeed a stumbling-block and to the
Gentiles foolishness, but to those who are called, both Jews
and Greeks, Christ, the power of God and the wisdom of

God. For the foolishness of God is wiser than men, and the weakness of God is stronger than men.

For consider your own call, brethren; that there were not many wise according to the flesh, not many mighty, not many noble. But the foolish things of the world has God chosen to put to shame the "wise," and the weak things of the world has God chosen to put to shame the strong, and the base things of the world and the despised has God chosen, and the things that are not, to bring to naught the things that are; lest any flesh should pride itself before him. From him you are in Christ Jesus, who has become for us God-given wisdom, and justice, and sanctification, and redemption; so that, just as it is written, "Let him who takes pride, take pride in the Lord."

And I, brethren, when I came to you, did not come with pretentious speech or wisdom, announcing unto you the witness to Christ. For I determined not to know anything among you, except Jesus Christ and him crucified. And I was with you in weakness and in fear and in much trembling. And my speech and my preaching were not in the persuasive words of wisdom, but in the demonstration of the Spirit and of power, that your faith might rest, not on the wisdom of men, but on the power of God.

Wisdom however, we speak among those who are mature, yet not a wisdom of this world nor of the rulers of this world, who are passing away. But we speak the wisdom of God, mysterious, hidden, which God foreordained before the world unto our glory, a wisdom which none of the rulers of this world has known; for had they known it, they would never have crucified the Lord of glory. But, as it is written, "Eye has not seen nor ear heard, nor has it entered into the heart of man, what things God has prepared for those who love him." But to us God has revealed them through his Spirit. For the Spirit searches all things, even the deep things of God. For who among men knows the things of a man save the spirit of the man which is in him? Even so, the things of God no one knows but the Spirit of God. Now we have received not the spirit of the world, but the spirit that is from God, that we may know the things that have been given us by God. These things we also speak, not in words taught by human wisdom, but in the learning of the Spirit, combining spiritual with spiritual. But the sensual man does not perceive the things that are of the Spirit of God, for it is foolishness to him and he cannot understand, because it is examined spiritually. But the spiritual man judges all things, and he himself is judged by no man. For "who has known the mind of the Lord, that he might instruct him?" But we have the mind of Christ.

And I, brethren, could not speak to you as to spiritual men but only as carnal, as to little children in Christ. I fed you with mild, not with solid food, for you were not yet ready for it. Nor are you now ready for it, for you are still carnal. For since there are jealousy and strife among you, are you not carnal, and walking as mere men? For whenever one says, "I am of Paul," but another, "I am of Apollos," are you not mere men?

What then is Apollos? What indeed is Paul? They are the servants of him whom you have believed—servants according as God has given to each to serve. I have planted, Apollos watered, but God has given the growth. So then neither he who plants is anything, nor he who waters, but God who gives the growth. Now he who plants and he who waters are one, yet each will receive his own reward according to his labor. For we are God's helpers, you are God's tillage, God's building.

According to the grace of God which has been given to me, as a wise builder, I laid the foundation, and another builds thereon. But let everyone take care how he builds thereon. For other foundation no one can lay, but that which has been laid, which is Christ Jesus. But if anyone builds upon this foundation, gold, silver, precious stones, wood, hay, straw—the work of each will be made manifest, for the day of the Lord will declare it, since the day is to be revealed in fire. The fire will assay the quality of everyone's work: if his work abides which he has built thereon, he will receive reward; if his work burns he will lose his reward, but himself will be saved, yet so as through fire.

Do you not know that you are the temple of God and that the Spirit of God dwells in you? If anyone destroys the temple of God, him will God destroy; for holy is the temple of God, and this temple you are.

Let no one deceive himself. If any one of you thinks himself wise in this world, let him become a fool, that he may come to be wise. For the wisdom of this world is foolishness with God. For it is written, "I will catch the wise in their craftiness." And again, "The Lord knows the thoughts of the wise, that they are empty." Therefore let no one take pride in men. For all things are yours, whether Paul, or Apollos, or Cephas; or the world, or life, or death; or things present, or things to come—all are yours, and you are Christ's, and Christ is God's.

Let a man so account us, as servants of Christ and stewards of the mysteries of God. Now here it is required in stewards that a man be found trustworthy. But with me it is a very small matter to be judged by you or by man's tribunal. Nay I do not even judge my own self. For I have nothing on my conscience, yet I am not thereby justified; but he who judges me is the Lord. Therefore, pass no judgment before the time, until the Lord comes, who will both bring to light the things hidden in darkness and make manifest the counsels of hearts; and then everyone will have his praise from God.

Now, brethren, I have applied these things to myself and Apollos by way of illustration for your sakes, that in our case you may learn not to be puffed up one against the other over a third party, transgressing what is written. For who singles thee out? Or what hast thou that thou hast not received? And if thou hast received it, why dost thou boast as if thou hadst not received it? You are already filled! You are already made rich! Without us you reign! And would that you did reign, that we too might reign with you! For I think God has set forth us the apostles last of all, as men doomed to death, seeing that we have been made a spectacle to the world, and to angels, and to men. We are fools for Christ, but you are wise in Christ! We are weak, but you are strong! You are honored, but we are without honor! To this very hour we hunger and thirst, and we are naked and buffeted, and have no fixed abode. And we toil, working with our own hands. We are reviled and we bless, we are persecuted and we bear with it, we are maligned and we entreat, we have become as the refuse of this world, the offscouring of all, even until now!

I write these things not to put you to shame, but to admonish you as my dearest children. For although you have ten thousand tutors in Christ, yet you have not many fathers. For in Christ Jesus, through the gospel, did I beget you. Therefore, I beg you, be imitators of me, as I am of Christ. For this very reason I have sent to you Timothy, who is my dearest son and faithful in the Lord. He will remind you of my ways, which are in Christ Jesus, even as I teach everywhere in every church.

Now some are puffed up, as if I were not coming to you. But I shall come to you shortly, if the Lord is willing, and I shall learn the power of those who are puffed up, not the promises. For the kingdom of God is not in word, but in power. What is your wish? Shall I come to you with a rod, or in love and in the spirit of meekness?

II. MORAL DISORDERS

It is actually reported that there is immorality among you, and such immorality as is not found even among the Gentiles, that a man should have his father's wife. And you are puffed up, and have not rather mourned so that he who has done this deed might be put away from your midst. I indeed, absent in body but present in spirit, have already, as though present, passed judgment in the name of our Lord Jesus Christ on the one who has so acted—you and my spirit gathered together with the power of our Lord Jesus—to deliver such a one over to Satan for the destruction of the flesh, that his spirit may be saved in the day of our Lord Jesus Christ. Your boasting is unseemly. Do you not know that a little leaven ferments the whole lump? Purge out the old leaven, that you may be a new dough, as you really are without leaven. For Christ, our passover, has been sacrificed. Therefore let us keep festival, not with the old leaven, not with the leaven of malice and wickedness, but with the unleavened bread of sincerity and truth.

I wrote to you in the letter not to associate with the immoral—not meaning, of course, the immoral of this world, or the covetous, or the greedy, or idolators; otherwise you would have to leave the world. But now I write to you not to associate with one who is called a brother, if he is immoral, or covetous, or an idolator, or evil-tongued, or a drunkard, or greedy; with such a one not even to take food. For what have I to do with judging those outside? Is it not those inside whom you judge? For those outside God will judge. "Expel the wicked man from your midst."

Dare any of you, having a matter against another, bring your case to be judged before the unjust and not before the saints? Do you not know that the saints will judge the world? And if the world will be judged by you, are you unworthy to judge the smallest matter? Do you not know that we shall judge angels? How much more worldly things! If, therefore, you have cases about worldly matters to be judged, appoint those who are rated as nothing in the Church to judge. To shame you I say it. Can it be that there is not one wise man among you competent to settle a case in his brother's matter? But brother goes to law with brother and that before unbelievers.

Nay, to begin with, it is altogether a defect in you that you have lawsuits one with another. Why not rather suffer wrong? Why not rather be defrauded? But you yourselves do wrong and defraud, and that to your brethren. Or do you not know that the unjust will not possess the kingdom of God? Do not err; neither fornicators, nor idolators, nor adulterers, nor the effeminate, nor sodomites, nor thieves, nor the covetous, nor drunkards, nor the evil-tongued, nor the greedy will possess the kingdom of God. And such were some of you, but you have been washed, you have been sanctified, you have been justified in the name of our Lord Jesus Christ, and in the Spirit of our God.

All things are lawful for me, but not all things are expedient. All things are lawful for me, but I will not be brought under the power of anyone. Food for the belly and the belly for food, but God will destroy both the one and the other. Now the body is not for immorality, but for the Lord, and the Lord for the body. Now God has raised up the Lord and will also raise us up by his power. Do you not know that your bodies are members of Christ? Shall I then take the members of Christ and make them members of a harlot? By no means! Or do you not know that he who cleaves to a harlot, becomes one body with her? "For the two," it says, "shall be one flesh." But he who cleaves to the Lord is one spirit with him. Flee immorality. Every sin that a man commits is outside the body, but the immoral man sins against his own body. Or do you not know that your members are the temple of the Holy Spirit, who is in you, whom you have from God, and that you are not your own? For you have been bought at a great price. Glorify God and bear him in your body.

III. ANSWERS TO QUESTIONS

Now concerning the things whereof you wrote to me: It is good for man not to touch woman. Yet, for fear of fornication, let each man have his own wife, and let each woman have her own husband. Let the husband render to the wife her due, and likewise the wife to the husband. The wife has not authority over her body, but the husband; the husband likewise has not authority over his body, but the wife. Do not deprive each other, except perhaps by consent, for a time, that you may give yourselves to prayer; and return together again lest Satan tempt you because you lack self-control. But this I say by way of concession, not by way of commandment. For I would that you all were as I am myself; but each one has his own gift from God, one in this way, and another in that.

But I say to the unmarried and to widows, it is good for them if they so remain, even as I. But if they do not have self-control, let them marry, for it is better to marry than to burn. But to those who are married, not I, but the Lord commands that a wife is not to depart from her husband, and if she departs, that she is to remain unmarried or be reconciled to her husband. And let not a husband put away his wife.

To the others I say, not the Lord: If any brother has an unbelieving wife and she consents to live with him, let him not put her away. And if any woman has an unbelieving husband and he consents to live with her, let her not put away her husband. For the unbelieving husband is sanctified by the believing wife, and the unbelieving wife is sanctified by the believing husband; otherwise your children would be unclean, but, as it is, they are holy. But if the unbeliever departs, let him depart. For a brother or sister is not under bondage in such cases, but God has called us to peace. For how dost thou know, O wife, whether thou wilt save thy husband? Or how dost thou know, O husband, whether thou wilt save thy wife?

Only, as the Lord has allotted to each, as when God has called each, so let him walk—and so I teach in all the churches. Was one called having been circumcised? Let him not become uncircumcised. Was one called being uncircumcised? Let him not be circumcised. Circumcision does not matter, and uncircumcision does not matter; but the keeping of the commandments of God is what matters. Let every man remain in the calling in which he was called. Wast thou a slave when called? Let it not trouble thee. But if thou canst become free, make use of it rather. For a slave who has been called in the Lord, is a freeman of the Lord; just as a freeman who has been called is a slave of Christ. You have been bought with a price; do not become the slaves of men. Brethren, in the state in which he was when called, let every man remain with God.

Now concerning virgins I have no commandment of the Lord, yet I give an opinion, as one having obtained mercy from the Lord to be trustworthy. I think, then, that this is good on account of the present distress—that it is good for a man to remain as he is. Art thou bound to a wife? Do not seek to be freed. Art thou freed from a wife? Do not seek a wife. But if thou takest a wife, thou hast not sinned. And if a virgin marries, she has not sinned. Yet such will have tribulation of the flesh. But I spare you that.

But this I say, brethren, the time is short; it remains that those who have wives be as if they had none; and those who weep, as though not weeping; and those who rejoice, as though not rejoicing; and those who buy, as though not possessing; and those who use this world, as though not using it, for this world as we see it is passing away. I would have you free from care. He who is unmarried is concerned about the things of the Lord, how he may please God. Whereas he who is married is concerned about the things of the world, how he may please his wife; and he is divided. And the unmarried woman, and the virgin, thinks about the things of the Lord, that she may be holy in body and in spirit. Whereas she who is married thinks about the things of the world, how she may please her husband. Now this I say for your benefit, not to hold you in check, but to promote what is proper, and to make it possible for you to pray to the Lord without distraction.

But if any man thinks that he incurs disgrace with regard to his virgin, since she is over age, and that it ought so to be done, let him do what he will; he does not sin if she should marry. But he who stands firm in his heart, being under no constraint, but is free to carry out his own will, and has decided to keep his virgin—he does well. Therefore both he who gives his virgin in marriage does well, and he who does not give her does better.

A woman is bound as long as her husband is alive, but if her husband dies, she is free. Let her marry whom she pleases, only let it be in the Lord. But she will be more blessed, in my judgment, if she remains as she is. And I think that I also have the spirit of God.

Now concerning things sacrificed to idols, we know that we all have knowledge. Knowledge puffs up, but charity edifies. If anyone thinks that he knows anything, he has not yet known as he ought to know. But if anyone loves God, the same is known by him. Now as for food sacrificed to idols, we know that there is no such thing as an idol in the world, and that there is no God but one. For even if there are what are called gods, whether in heaven or on earth (for indeed there are many gods, and many lords), yet for us there is only one God, the Father from whom are all things, and we unto him; and one Lord, Jesus Christ, through whom are all things, and we through him.

But such knowledge is not in everyone. Some, still idol-conscious, eat idol offerings as such, and their conscience, being weak, is defiled. Now food does not commend us to God. For neither shall we suffer any loss if we do not eat, nor if we do eat shall we have any advantage. Still, take care lest perhaps this right of yours become a stumbling-block to the weak. For if a man sees one who "has knowledge" reclining at table in an idol place, will not his conscience, weak as it is, be emboldened to eat idol-offerings? And through thy "knowledge" the weak one will perish, the brother for whom Christ died. Now when you sin thus against the brethren, and wound their weak conscience, you sin against Christ. Therefore, if food scandalizes my brother, I will eat flesh no more forever, lest I scandalize my brother.

Am I not free? Am I not an apostle? Have I not seen Jesus our Lord? Are not you my work in the Lord? And if to others I am not an apostle, yet to you I am. For you are the seal set upon my apostleship in the Lord. My defense against those who question me is this: Have we not a right to eat and to drink? Have we not a right to take about with us a woman, a sister, as do the other apostles, and the brethren of the Lord, and Cephas? Or is it only Barnabas and I who have not the right to do this? What soldier ever serves at his own expense? Who plants a vineyard and does not eat of its fruit? Who feeds the flock, and does not eat of the milk of the flock? Do I speak these things on human authority? Or does not the Law also say these things? For it is written in the Law of Moses, "Thou shalt not muzzle the ox that treads out the grain." Is it for the oxen that God has care? Or does he say this simply for our sakes? These things were written for us. For he who plows should plow in hope, and he who threshes, in hope of partaking of the fruits. If we have sown for you spiritual things, is it a great matter if we reap from you carnal things? If others share in this right over you, why not we rather? But we have not used this right, but we bear all things, lest we offer hindrance to the gospel of Christ. Do you not know that they who minister in the temple eat what comes from the temple, and that they who serve the altar, have their share with the altar? So also the Lord directed that those who preach the gospel should have their living from the gospel.

But I for my part have used none of these rights. Neither do I write these things that so it should be done in my case. For it were better for me to die than that anyone should make void my boast. For even if I preach the gospel, I have therein no ground for boasting, since I am under constraint. For woe to me if I do not preach the gospel! If I do this willingly, I have a reward. But if unwillingly, it is a stewardship that has been entrusted to me. What then is my reward? That preaching the gospel, I deliver the gospel without charge, so as not to abuse my right in the gospel.

For, free though I was as to all, unto all I have made myself a slave that I might gain the more converts. And I have become to the Jews a Jew that I might gain the Jews; to those under the Law, as one under the Law (though not myself under the Law), that I might gain those under the Law; to

52

those without the Law, as one without the Law (though I am not without the law of God, but am under the law of Christ), that I might gain those without the Law. To the weak I became weak, that I might gain the weak. I became all things to all men, that I might save all. I do all things for the sake of the gospel, that I may be made partaker thereof.

Do you not know that those who run in a race, all indeed run, but one receives the prize? So run as to obtain it. And everyone in a contest abstains from all things—and they indeed to receive a perishable crown, but we an imperishable. I, therefore, so run as not without a purpose; I so fight as not beating the air; but I chastise my body and bring it into subjection, lest perhaps after preaching to others I myself should be rejected.

For I would not have you ignorant, brethren, that our fathers were all under the cloud, and all passed through the sea, and all were baptized in Moses, in the cloud and in the sea. And all ate the same spiritual food, and all drank the same spiritual drink (for they drank from the spiritual rock which followed them, and the rock was Christ). Yet with most of them God was not well pleased, for "they were laid low in the desert."

Now these things came to pass as examples to us, that we should not lust after evil things even as they lusted. And do not become idolators, even as some of them were, as it is written, "The people sat down to eat and drink, and rose up to play." Neither let us commit fornication, even as some of them committed fornication, and there fell in one day twenty-three thousand. Neither let us tempt Christ, as some of them tempted, and perished by the serpents. Neither murmur, as some of them murmured, and perished at the hands of the destroyer. Now all these things happened to them as a type, and they were written for our correction, upon whom the final age of the world has come.

Therefore let him who thinks he stands take heed lest he fall. May no temptation take hold of you but such as man is equal to. God is faithful and will not permit you to be tempted beyond your strength, but with the temptation will also give you a way out that you may be able to bear it.

Therefore, beloved, flee from the worship of idols. I am speaking as to men of sense; judge for yourselves what I say. The cup of blessing that we bless, is it not the sharing of the blood of Christ? And the bread that we break, is it not the partaking of the body of the Lord? Because the bread is one, we though many, are one body, all of us who partake of the one bread. Behold Israel according to the flesh, are not they who eat of the sacrifices partakers of the altar? What then do I say? That what is sacrificed to idols is anything, or that an idol is anything? No; but I say that what the Gentiles sacrifice, "they sacrifice to devils and not to God"; and I would not have you become associates of devils. You cannot drink the cup of the Lord and the cup of devils; you cannot be partakers of the table of the Lord and of the table of devils. Or are we provoking the Lord to jealousy? Are we stronger than he?

All things are lawful, but not all things are expedient. All things are lawful, but not all things edify. Let no one seek his own interests, but those of his neighbor. Anything that is sold in the market, eat, asking no question for conscience' sake. "The earth is the Lord's, and the fullness thereof." If one of the unbelievers invites you, and you wish to go, eat whatever is set before you, and ask no question for

conscience' sake. But if someone says, "This has been sacrificed to idols," do not eat of it, for the sake of him who told
you and for conscience' sake—I mean the other's conscience,
not thine. For why should my liberty be called to judgment
by another's conscience? If I partake with thanksgiving, why
am I ill spoken of for that for which I give thanks?

Therefore, whether you eat or drink, or do anything else,
do all for the glory of God. Do not be a stumbling-block to
Jews and Greeks and to the church of God, even as I myself
in all things please all men, not seeking what is profitable to
myself but to the many, that they may be saved.

Be imitators of me as I am of Christ.

IV. RELIGIOUS GATHERINGS

Now I praise you, brethren, because in all things you are
mindful of me and hold fast my precepts as I gave them
to you. But I would have you know that the head of every
man is Christ, and the head of the woman is the man, and
the head of Christ is God. Every man praying or prophesying with his head covered, disgraces his head. But every
woman praying or prophesying with her head uncovered
disgraces her head, for it is the same as if she were shaven.
For if a woman is not covered, let her be shaven. But if it
is a disgrace for a woman to have her hair cut off or her
head shaven, let her cover her head. A man indeed ought
not to cover his head, because he is the image and glory of
God. But woman is the glory of man. For man is not from
woman, but woman from man. For man was not created
for woman, but woman for man. This is why the woman

ought to have a sign of authority over her head, because of the angels.

Yet neither is man independent of woman, nor woman independent of man in the Lord. For as the woman is from the man, so also is the man through the woman, but all things are from God. Judge for yourselves: does it become a woman to pray to God uncovered? Does not nature itself teach you that for a man to wear his hair long is degrading; but for a woman to wear her hair long is a glory to her? Because her hair has been given her as a covering. But if anyone is disposed to be contentious—we have no such custom, neither have the churches of God.

But in giving this charge, I do not commend you in that you meet not for the better but for the worse. For first of all I hear that when you meet in church there are divisions among you, and in part I believe it. For there must be factions, so that those who are approved may be made manifest among you. So then when you meet together, it is no longer possible to eat the Lord's Supper. For at the meal, each one takes first his own supper, and one is hungry, and another drinks overmuch. Have you not houses for your eating and drinking? Or do you despise the church of God and put to shame the needy? What am I to say to you? Am I to commend you? In this I do not commend you.

For I myself have received from the Lord (what I also delivered to you), that the Lord Jesus, on the night in which he was betrayed, took bread, and giving thanks broke, and said, "This is my body which shall be given up for you; do this in remembrance of me." In like manner also the cup, after he had supped, saying, "This cup is the new covenant in my blood; do this as often as you drink it, in remembrance of me. For as often as you shall eat this bread and drink the cup, you proclaim the death of the Lord, until he comes." Therefore whoever eats this bread or drinks the cup of the Lord unworthily, will be guilty of the body and the blood of the Lord. But let a man prove himself, and so let him eat of that bread and drink of the cup; for he who eats and drinks unworthily, without distinguishing the body, eats and drinks judgment to himself. This is why many among you are infirm and weak, and many sleep. But if we judged ourselves, we should not thus be judged. But when we are judged, we are being chastised by the Lord that we may not be condemned with this world. Wherefore, my brethren, when you come together to eat, wait for one another. If anyone is hungry, let him eat at home, lest you come together unto judgment. The rest I shall set in order when I come.

V. THE SPIRITUAL GIFTS

Now concerning spiritual gifts, brethren, I would not have you ignorant. You know that when you were Gentiles, you went to dumb idols according as you were led. Wherefore I give you to understand that no one speaking in the Spirit of God says "Anathema" to Jesus. And no one can say "Jesus is Lord," except in the Holy Spirit.

Now there are varieties of gifts, but the same Spirit; and there are varieties of ministries, but the same Lord; and there are varieties of workings, but the same God, who works all things in all. Now the manifestation of the Spirit is given to everyone for profit. To one through the Spirit is given the utterance of wisdom; and to another the utterance of knowledge, according to the same Spirit; to another faith, in the same Spirit; to another the gift of healing, in the one Spirit; to another the working of miracles; to another prophecy; to another the distinguishing of spirits; to another various kinds of tongues; to another interpretation of tongues. But all these things are the work of one and the same Spirit, who allots to everyone according as he will.

For as the body is one and has many members, and all the members of the body, many as they are, form one body, so also is it with Christ.

For in one Spirit we were all baptized into one body, whether Jews or Gentiles, whether slave or free; and we were all given to drink of one Spirit. For the body is not one member, but many. If the foot says, "Because I am not a hand, I am not of the body," is it therefore not of the body? And if the ear says, "Because I am not an eye, I am not of the body," is it therefore not of the body?

If the whole body were an eye, where would be the hearing? If the whole body were hearing, where would be the smelling? But as it is, God has set the members, each of them, in the body as he willed. Now if they were all one member, where would the body be? But as it is, there are indeed many members, yet but one body. And the eye cannot say to the hand, "I do not need thy help"; nor again the head to the feet, "I have no need of you." Nay, much rather, those that seem the more feeble members of the body are more necessary; and those that we think the less honorable members of the body, we surround with more abundant honor, and our uncomely parts receive a more abundant comeliness, whereas our comely parts have no need of it. But God has so tempered the body together in due portion as to give more abundant honor where it was lacking; that there may be no disunion in the body, but that the members may have care for one another. And if one member suffers anything, all the members suffer with it, or if one member glories, all the members rejoice with it.

Now you are the body of Christ, member for member. And God indeed has placed some in the Church, first apostles, secondly prophets, thirdly teachers, after that miracles, then gifts of healing, services of help, power of administration, and the speaking of various tongues. Are all apostles? Are all prophets? Are all teachers? Are all workers of miracles? Do all have the gift of healing? Do all speak with tongues? Do all interpret? Yet strive after the greater gifts.

And I point out to you a yet more excellent way. If I speak with the tongues of man and of angels, but do not have charity, I have become as sounding brass or a tinkling cymbal. And if I have prophecy and know all mysteries and all knowledge, and if I have all faith so as to remove mountains, yet do not have charity, I am nothing. And if I distribute all my goods to feed the poor, and if I deliver my body to be burned, yet do not have charity, it profits me nothing.

Charity is patient, is kind; charity does not envy, is not pretentious, is not puffed up, is not ambitious, is not self-seeking, is not provoked; thinks no evil, does not rejoice over wickedness, but rejoices with the truth; bears with all things, believes all things, hopes all things, endures all things.

Charity never fails, whereas prophecies will disappear, and tongues will cease, and knowledge will be destroyed. For we know in part and we prophesy in part; but when that which is perfect has come, that which is imperfect will be done away with. When I was a child, I spoke as a child, I felt as a child, I thought as a child. Now that I have become a man, I have put away the things of a child. We see now through a mirror in an obscure manner, but then face to face. Now I know in part, but then I shall know even as I have been known. So there abide faith, hope and charity, these three; but the greatest of these is charity.

Aim at charity, yet strive after the spiritual gifts, but especially that you may prophesy. For he who speaks in a tongue does not speak to men but to God; for no one understands, as he is speaking mysteries in his spirit. But he who prophesies speaks to men for edification, and encouragement, and consolation. He who speaks in a tongue edifies himself, but he who prophesies edifies the church. Now I should like you all to speak in tongues, but still more to prophesy; for he who prophesies is greater than he who speaks in tongues, unless he can interpret so that the church may receive edification.

But now, brethren, if I come to you speaking in tongues what shall I profit you, unless I speak to you either in revelation, or in knowledge, or in prophecy, or in teaching? Even inanimate instruments, like the flute or the harp, may produce sound, but if there is no difference in the notes, how shall it be known what is piped or harped? If the trumpet give forth an uncertain sound, who will prepare for battle? So likewise you—unless with the tongue you utter intelligible speech—how shall it be known what is said? For you will be speaking to the empty air. There are, for example, so many kinds of languages in this world and none without a meaning. If, then, I do not know the meaning of the language, I shall be to the one to whom I speak, a foreigner;

and he who speaks, a foreigner to me. So also you, since you strive after spiritual gifts, seek to have them abundantly for the edification of the church.

Therefore let him who speaks in a tongue pray that he may interpret. For if I pray in a tongue, my spirit prays, but my understanding is unfruitful. What, then, is to be done? I will pray with the spirit, but I will pray with the understanding also; I will sing with the spirit, but I will sing with the understanding also. Else if thou givest praise with the spirit alone, how shall he who fills the place of the uninstructed say "Amen" to thy thanksgiving? For he does not know what thou sayest. For thou, indeed, givest thanks well, but the other is not edified. I thank God I speak with all your tongues; yet in the church, I had rather speak five words with my understanding, that I may also instruct others, than ten thousand words in a tongue.

Brethren, do not become children in mind, but in malice be children and in mind mature. In the Law it is written that "In other tongues and with other lips I will speak to this people, and not even so will they listen to me, says the Lord." Wherefore tongues are intended as a sign, not to believers, but to unbelievers; whereas prophecies, not to unbelievers, but to believers. Therefore, if the whole church be assembled together and, while all are speaking with tongues, there should come in uninstructed persons or unbelievers, will they not say that you are mad? Whereas, if while all are prophesying, there should come in an unbeliever or uninstructed person, he is convicted by all, he is put on trial by all; the secrets of his heart are made manifest, and so, falling on his face, he will worship God, declaring that God is truly among you.

What then is to be done, brethren? When you come together each of you has a hymn, has an instruction, has
a revelation, has a tongue, has an interpretation. Let all
things be done unto edification. If anyone speaks in a
tongue, let it be by twos or at most threes, and let them
speak in turn, and let one interpret. But if there is no in-
terpreter let him keep silence in the church, and speak to
himself and to God. Of the prophets, let two or three speak
at a meeting, and let the rest act as judges. But if anything
is revealed to another sitting by, let the first keep silence.
For you all can prophesy one by one, so that all may learn
and all may be encouraged. For the spirits of the prophets
are under the control of the prophets. For God is a God of
peace, not of disorder.

Thus I likewise teach in all the churches of the saints. Let
women keep silence in the churches, for it is not permitted
them to speak, but let them be submissive, as the Law also
says. But if they wish to learn anything let them ask their
husbands at home, for it is unseemly for a woman to speak
in church.

What, was it from you that the word of God went forth?
Or was it unto you only that it reached? If anyone thinks
that he is a prophet or spiritual, let him recognize that the
things I am writing to you are the Lord's commandments. If
anyone ignores this, he shall be ignored. So then, brethren,
desire earnestly the gift of prophesying and do not hinder
the gift of speaking in tongues. Only let all things be done
properly and in order.

VI. THE RESURRECTION

Now I recall to your minds, brethren, the gospel that I preached to you, which also you received, wherein also you stand, through which also you are being saved, if you hold it fast, as I preached it to you—unless you have believed to no purpose. For I delivered, that Christ died for our sins according to the Scriptures, and that he was buried, and that he rose again the third day, according to the Scriptures, and that he appeared to Cephas, and after that to the Eleven. Then he was seen by more than five hundred brethren at one time, many of whom are with us still, but some have fallen asleep. After that he was seen by James, then by all the apostles. And last of all, as by one born out of due time, he was seen also by me. For I am the least of the apostles, and am not worthy to be called an apostle, because I persecuted the Church of God. But by the grace of God I am what I am, and his grace in me has not been fruitless—in fact I have labored more than any of them, yet not I, but the grace of God with me. Whether then it is I or they, so we preach, and so you have believed.

Now if Christ is preached as risen from the dead, how do some among you say that there is no resurrection of the dead? But if there is no resurrection of the dead, neither has Christ risen; and if Christ has not risen, vain then is our preaching, vain too is your faith. Yes, and we are found false witnesses as to God, in that we have borne witness against God that he raised Christ—whom he did not raise, if the dead do not rise. For if the dead do not rise, neither has Christ risen; and if Christ has not risen, vain is your faith, for you are still in your sins. Hence they also who have fallen asleep in Christ, have perished. If with this life only in view we have had hope in Christ, we are of all men the most to be pitied.

But as it is, Christ has risen from the dead, the first-fruits of those who have fallen asleep. For since by a man came death, by a man also comes resurrection of the dead.

For as in Adam all die, so in Christ all will be made to live. But each in his own turn, Christ as first-fruits, then they who are Christ's, who have believed, at his coming. Then comes the end, when he delivers the kingdom to God the Father, when he does away with all sovereignty, authority and power. For he must reign, until "he has put all his enemies under his feet." And the last enemy to be destroyed will be death, for "he has put all things under his feet." But when he says all things are subject to him, undoubtedly he is excepted who has subjected all things to him. And when all things are made subject to him, then the Son himself will also be made subject to him who subjected all things to him, that God may be all in all.

Else what shall they do who receive Baptism for the dead? If the dead do not rise at all, why then do people receive Baptism for them? And we, why do we stand in jeopardy every hour? I die daily, I affirm it, by the very pride that I take in you, brethren, in Christ Jesus our Lord. If, as men do, I fought with beasts at Ephesus, what does it profit me? If the dead do not rise, "let us eat and drink for tomorrow we shall die." Do not be led astray, "evil companionships corrupt good morals." Awake as you should, and do not sin; for some have no knowledge of God. To your shame I say so.

But someone will say, "How do the dead rise? Or with what kind of body do they come?" Senseless man, what thou thyself sowest is not brought to life, unless it dies. And when thou sowest, thou dost not sow the body that shall be, but a bare grain, perhaps of wheat or something else. But God gives it a body even as he has willed, and to each of the seeds a body of its own. All flesh is not the same flesh, but here is one flesh of man, another of beasts, another of birds, another of fishes. There are also heavenly bodies and earthly bodies, but of one kind is the glory of the heavenly, of another kind the glory of the earthly. There is one glory of the sun, and another glory of the moon, and another of the stars; for star differs from star in glory. So also with the resurrection of the dead. What is sown in corruption rises in incorruption; What is sown in dishonor rises in glory; what is sown in weakness rises in power; what is sown a natural body rises a spiritual body.

If there is a natural body, there is also a spiritual body. So also it is written, "The first man, Adam, became a living soul"; the last Adam became a life-giving spirit. But it is not the spiritual that comes first, but the physical, and then the spiritual. The first man was of the earth, earthy; the second man is from heaven, heavenly. As was the earthy man, such also are the earthy; and as is the heavenly man, such also are the heavenly. Therefore, even as we have borne the likeness of the earthy, let us bear also the likeness of the heavenly.

Now this I say, brethren, that flesh and blood can obtain no part in the kingdom of God, neither shall corruption have any part in incorruption. Behold, I tell you a mystery: we shall all indeed rise, but we shall not all be changed—in a moment, in the twinkling of an eye, at the last trumpet. For the trumpet shall sound, and the dead shall rise incorruptible and we shall be changed. For this corruptible body must put on incorruption, and this mortal body must put on immortality. But when this mortal body puts on immortality, then shall come to pass the word that is written, "Death is swallowed up in victory! O death, where is thy victory? O death, where is thy sting?"

Now the sting of death is sin, and the power of sin is the Law. But thanks be to God who has given us the victory through our Lord Jesus Christ.

Therefore, my beloved brethren, be steadfast and immovable, always abounding in the work of the Lord, knowing that your labor is not in vain in the Lord.

Now concerning the collection being made for the saints, as I have ordered the churches of Galatia, do you also. On the first day of the week, let each one of you put aside at home and lay up whatever he has a mind to, so that the collections may not have to be made after I have come. But when I am with you, whomever you may authorize by giving credentials, them I will send to carry your gift to Jerusalem. And if it is important enough for me also to go, they shall go with me.

But I shall come to you after passing through Macedonia (for I mean to pass through Macedonia); but with you I shall perhaps remain or even winter, so that you may speed me wherever I may be going. For I do not wish to see you just now in passing by, for I hope to stay some time with you, if the Lord permits. But I shall stay on at Ephesus until Pentecost. For a door has been opened to me, great and evident, and there are many adversaries.

Now if Timothy comes, see that he be with you without fear, for he works the work of the Lord just as I do. Therefore, let no one despise him, but speed him on his way in peace that he may come to me, for I am awaiting him with the brethren.

With regard to our brother Apollos, I earnestly besought him to come to you with the brethren, and he was quite unwilling to come at present; but he will come when he has leisure.

Watch, stand fast in the faith, act like men, be strong. Let all that you do be done in charity. Now I beseech you, brethren—you know that the household of Stephanas and of Fortunatus are the first-fruits of Achaia, and have devoted themselves to the service of the saints—to such as these do you also be subject, and to every helper and worker. I rejoice at the presence of Stephanas and Fortunatus and Achaicus, because what was lacking on your part they have supplied; for they have refreshed both my spirit and yours. To such as these, therefore, give recognition.

The churches of Asia greet you. Aquila and Priscilla with the church at their house greet you heartily in the Lord. All the brethren greet you. Greet one another with a holy kiss.

I Paul greet you, with my own hand. If any man does not love the Lord Jesus Christ, let him be anathema. Maranatha. The grace of our Lord Jesus Christ be with you. My love is with you all in Christ Jesus. Amen.

A *Note about*
The Second Epistle of St. Paul the Apostle
to the Corinthians

St. Paul wrote this second canonical Epistle to the Christians of Corinth from Macedonia towards the close of his third missionary journey, and therefore very probably around the year 57 of our era. The Apostle had lately come from Ephesus, where he had spent over two years, and was on his way to Corinth. He had previously sent Titus to Corinth to visit the new community and to ascertain the effect on the faithful there of a severe letter which he had been obliged to write them some time before.

Paul and Titus had first arranged to meet at Troas, a Mysian seaport on the eastern shore of the Aegean Sea; but St. Paul arrived there ahead of schedule, and being anxious for news from Corinth, went across the sea to Philippi in Macedonia, and it was probably there that he met his envoy.

The report given by Titus of the effect on the Corinthians of St. Paul's letter from Ephesus occasioned this Epistle, in which the Apostle defends his life and ministry, urges that the collection—already requested and begun—be made for the poor Christians in Jerusalem, and replies to his bitter opponents. The Epistle ranks with those to Timothy and the Galatians as the most intensely personal of St. Paul's writings. But unlike the letters to Timothy, which are calmly pastoral and directive, this Epistle is vehement and hotly polemical, especially in the four closing chapters. The writer will have his critics and adversaries understand that he is a true apostle of Jesus Christ, and that his sincerity and authority have been amply attested by extraordinary visitations from heaven and by unparalleled labors and sufferings on behalf of the Gospel.

The Second Epistle of St. Paul the Apostle to the Corinthians

INTRODUCTION

Paul, an apostle of Jesus Christ by the will of God, and Timothy our brother, to the church of God that is at Corinth, with all the saints that are in the whole of Achaia: grace be to you and peace from God our Father and from the Lord Jesus Christ.

Blessed be the God and Father of our Lord Jesus Christ, the Father of mercies and the God of all comfort, who comforts us in all our afflictions, that we also may be able to comfort those who are in any distress by the comfort wherewith we ourselves are comforted by God. For as the sufferings of Christ abound in us, so also through Christ does our comfort abound. For whether we are afflicted, it is for your instruction and salvation; or whether we are comforted, it is for your comfort; which shows its efficacy in the endurance of the selfsame sufferings that we also suffer. And our hope for you is steadfast, knowing that as you are partakers of the sufferings, so will you also be of the comfort.

For we would not, brethren, have you ignorant of the

affliction which came upon us in Asia. We were crushed beyond measure—beyond our strength, so that we were weary even of life. Yes, we have been carrying, within our very selves, our death sentence; in order that we may not trust in ourselves, but in God who raises the dead. He it is who delivered us, and will deliver us, from such great perils; and in him we have hope to be delivered yet again, through the help of your prayers for us. Thus, for the gift bestowed on us at the instance of many persons, thanks will be given by many on our behalf.

For our boast is this, the testimony of our conscience that in simplicity and godly sincerity—not in carnal wisdom, but in the grace of God—we have conducted ourselves in the world, and especially in our relations with you. For we write nothing to you that you do not read and understand. Indeed, I hope you will always understand, even as you have understood us in part, that we are your boast, as you will also be ours, in the day of our Lord Jesus Christ.

I. PERSONAL DEFENSE

With this assurance I meant, in order that you might enjoy a double grace, to visit you first, and to pass through you into Macedonia, and from Macedonia to come again to you, and by you to be sent forward on my way to Judea. Now in this my intention, did I show fickleness? Or are my plans made according to the flesh, so that with me it is now "Yes" and now "No"? God is my witness that our message to you is not both "Yes" and "No." For the Son of God, Jesus Christ, who was preached among you by us—by me and Silvanus and Timothy—was not now "Yes" and now "No," but only "Yes" was in him. For all the promises of God find their "Yes" in him; and therefore through him also rises the "Amen" to God unto our glory. Now it is God who is warrant for us and for you in Christ, who has anointed us, who has also stamped us with his seal and has given us the Spirit as a pledge in our hearts.

Now I call God to witness against my soul that it was to spare you that I did not again come to Corinth. Not that we lord it over your faith, but rather we are fellow-workers in your joy; for in faith you stand.

But I made up my mind not to come to you again in sorrow. For if I make you sad, who can gladden me, save the very one that is grieved by me? And I wrote to you as I did, that when I come I may not have sorrow upon sorrow from those who ought to give me joy; for I trust in you all that my joy is the joy of you all. For I wrote to you in much affliction and anguish of heart, with many tears, not that you might be grieved, but that you might know the great love I have for you.

Now if anyone has caused grief, he has not grieved me, but in a measure (not to be too severe) all of you. For such a one this punishment meted out by the many is sufficient. On the contrary, then, you should rather forgive and comfort him, lest perchance he be overwhelmed by too much sorrow. Therefore I exhort you to assure him of your love for him. For to this very end also did I write, that I might test you and know whether you are obedient in all things. Whom you pardon anything, I also pardon. Indeed, what I have forgiven—if I have forgiven anything—I have done for your sakes, in the person of Christ, that we may not be defeated by Satan; for we are not unaware of his devices.

Now when I came to Troas to preach the gospel of Christ, though I had there a great opportunity in the Lord, I had no peace of mind, because I did not find Titus my brother. And so, bidding them farewell, I went on to Macedonia. But thanks be to God, who always leads us in triumph in Christ Jesus, manifesting through us the odor of his knowledge in every place. For we are the fragrance of Christ for God, alike as regards those who are saved and those who are lost; to these an odor that leads to death, but to those an odor that leads to life. And for such offices, who is sufficient? We, at least, are not, as many others, adulterating the word of God; but with sincerity, as coming from God, we preach in Christ in God's presence.

Are we beginning again to commend ourselves? Or do we need, as some do, letters of commendation to you or from you? You are our letter, written on our hearts, which is known and read by all men; clearly you are a letter of Christ, composed by us, written not with ink but with the Spirit of the living God, not on tablets of stone but on fleshly tablets of the heart.

Such is the assurance I have through Christ towards God. Not that we are sufficient of ourselves to think anything, as from ourselves, but our sufficiency is from God. He also it is who has made us fit ministers of the new covenant, not of the letter but of the spirit; for the letter kills, but the spirit gives life.

Now if the ministration of death, which was engraved in letters upon stones, was inaugurated in such glory that the children of Israel could not look steadfastly upon the face of Moses on account of the transient glory that shone upon it, shall not the ministration of the spirit be still more glorious?

For if there is glory in the ministration that condemned, much more does the ministration that justifies abound in glory. For though the former ministration was gloried, yet in this regard it is without glory, because of the surpassing glory of the latter. For if that which was transient was glorious, much more is that glorious which abides.

Having therefore such hope, we show great boldness. We do not act as Moses did, who used to put a veil over his face that the Israelites might not observe the glory of his countenance, which was to pass away. But their minds were darkened; for to this day, when the Old Testament is read to them, the selfsame veil remains, not being lifted to disclose the Christ in whom it is made void. Yes, down to this very day, when Moses is read, the veil covers their hearts; but when they turn in repentance to God, the veil shall be taken away. Now the Lord is the spirit; and where the Spirit of the Lord is, there is freedom. But we all, with faces unveiled, reflecting as in a mirror the glory of the Lord, are being transformed into his very image from glory to glory, as through the Spirit of the Lord.

Discharging therefore this ministry in accordance with the mercy shown us, we do not lose heart. On the contrary, we renounce those practices which shame conceals, we avoid unscrupulous conduct, we do not corrupt the word of God; but making known the truth, we commend ourselves to every man's conscience in the sight of God. And if our gospel also is veiled, it is veiled only to those who are perishing. In their case, the god of this world has blinded their unbelieving minds, that they should not see the light of the gospel of the glory of Christ, who is the image of God. For we preach not ourselves, but Jesus Christ as Lord, and ourselves merely as your servants in Jesus. For God, who commanded light to shine out of darkness, has shone in our hearts, to give enlightenment concerning the knowledge of the glory of God, shining on the face of Christ Jesus.

But we carry this treasure in vessels of clay, to show that the abundance of the power is God's and not ours. In all things we suffer tribulation, but we are not distressed; we are sore pressed, but we are not destitute; we endure persecution, but we are not forsaken; we are cast down, but we do not perish; always bearing about in our body the dying of Jesus, so that the life also of Jesus may be made manifest in our bodily frame. For we the living are constantly being handed over to death for Jesus' sake, that the life also of Jesus may be made manifest in our mortal flesh. Thus death is at work in us, but life in you. But since we have the same spirit of faith, as shown in that which is written—"I believed, and so I spoke"—we also believed, wherefore we also spoke. For we know that he who raised up Jesus will raise up us also with Jesus, and will place us with you. For all things are for your sakes, so that the grace which abounds through the many may cause thanksgiving to abound, to the glory of God.

Wherefore we do not lose heart. On the contrary, even though our outer man is decaying, yet our inner man is being renewed day by day. For our present light affliction, which is for the moment, prepares for us an eternal weight of glory that is beyond all measure; while we look not at the things that are seen, but at the things that are not seen. For the things that are seen are temporal, but the things that are not seen are eternal.

For we know that if the earthly house in which we dwell be destroyed, we have a building from God, a house not made by human hands, eternal in the heavens. And indeed, in this present state we groan, yearning to be clothed over with that dwelling of ours which is from heaven; if indeed we shall be found clothed, and not naked. For we who are in this tent sigh under our burden, because we do not wish to be unclothed, but rather clothed over, that what is mortal may be swallowed up by life. Now he who made us for this very thing is God, who has given us the Spirit as its pledge.

Always full of courage, then, and knowing that while we are in the body we are exiled from the Lord—for we walk by faith and not by sight—we even have the courage to prefer to be exiled from the body and to be at home with the Lord. And therefore we strive, whether in the body or out of it, to be pleasing to him. For all of us must be made manifest before the tribunal of Christ, so that each one may receive what he has won through the body, according to his works, whether good or evil.

Knowing therefore the fear of the Lord, we try to persuade men; but to God we are manifest. And I hope also that in your consciences we are manifest.

We are not again commending ourselves to you; but we are giving you occasion to boast about us, that you may have an answer for them who glory in appearances and not in heart. For if we were out of our mind, it was for God; if we are sane, it is for you. For the love of Christ impels us, because we have come to the conclusion that, since one died for all, therefore all died; and that Christ died for all, in order that they who are alive may live no longer for themselves, but for him who died for them and rose again.

So that henceforth we know no one according to the flesh. And even though we have known Christ according to the flesh, yet now we know him so no longer. If then any man is in Christ, he is a new creature: the former things have passed away; behold, they are made new! But all things are from God, who has reconciled us to himself through Christ and has given to us the ministry of reconciliation.

For God was truly in Christ, reconciling the world to himself by not reckoning against men their sins and by entrusting to us the message of reconciliation.

On behalf of Christ, therefore, we are acting as ambassadors, God, as it were, appealing through us. We exhort you, for Christ's sake, be reconciled to God. For our sakes he made him to be sin who knew nothing of sin, so that in him we might become the justice of God.

Yes, working together with him we entreat you not to receive the grace of God in vain. For he says, "In an acceptable time I have heard thee, and in the day of salvation I have helped thee." Behold now is the acceptable time; behold, now is the day of salvation! We give no offense to anyone, that our ministry may not be blamed. On the contrary, let us conduct ourselves in all circumstances as God's ministers, in much patience; in tribulations, in hardships, in distresses; in stripes, in imprisonments, in tumults; in labors, in sleepless nights, in fastings; in innocence, in knowledge, in long-sufferings; in kindness, in the Holy Spirit, in unaffected love; in the word of truth, in the power of God; with the armor of justice on the right hand and on the left; in honor and dishonor, in evil report and good report; as deceivers and yet truthful, as unknown and yet well known, as dying and behold, we live, as chastised but not killed, as sorrowful yet always rejoicing, as poor yet enriching many, as having nothing yet possessing all things.

We are frank with you, O Corinthians; our heart is wide open to you. In us there is no lack of room for you, but in your heart there is no room for us. Now as having a recompense in like kind—I speak as to my children—be you also open wide to us.

Do not bear the yoke with unbelievers. For what has justice in common with iniquity? Or what fellowship has light with darkness? What harmony is there between Christ and Belial? Or what part has the believer with the unbeliever? And what agreement has the temple of God with idols? For you are the temple of the living God, as God says, "I will dwell and move among them, I will be their God and they shall be my people." Wherefore, "Come out from among them, be separated, says the Lord, and touch not an unclean thing; and I will welcome you in, and will be a Father to you, and you shall be my sons and daughters, says the Lord almighty."

Having therefore these promises, beloved, let us cleanse ourselves from all defilement of the flesh and of the spirit, perfecting holiness in the fear of God.

Make room for us. We have wronged no one, we have corrupted no one, we have taken advantage of no one. I am not saying this to condemn you; for I have already said that you are in our hearts, to die together and to live together. Great is my confidence in you, great my boasting about you. I am filled with comfort, I overflow with joy in all our troubles.

For indeed when we came to Macedonia, our flesh had no rest; we had troubles on every side, conflicts without and anxieties within. But God, who comforts the humble, comforted us by the arrival of Titus. And not by his arrival only, but also by the comfort which he himself experienced in you. He told us of your longing, of your sorrow, of your zeal for me, so that I rejoiced yet more.

Wherefore, although I made you sorry by my letter, I do not regret it. And even if I did regret it, seeing that the same letter did for a while make you sorry, now I am glad; not because you were made sorry, but because your sorrow led you to repentance. For you were made sorry according to God, that you might suffer no loss at our hands. For the sorrow that is according to God produces repentance that surely tends to salvation, whereas the sorrow that is according to the world produces death. For behold this very fact that you were made sorry according to God, what earnestness it has wrought in you, nay, what explanations, what indignation, what fear, what yearning, what zeal, what readiness to avenge! In everything you have showed yourselves to be innocent in the matter.

If then I did write to you, it was not for the sake of him who did the wrong, not for the sake of him who suffered the wrong; but to make clear the zeal we have for you, before God. This is why we have been comforted. But besides our own comfort, we more especially rejoiced at the joy of Titus, because his mind had been set at rest by you all. And if I did boast to him at all about you, I have not been put to shame; but just as we have spoken all things in truth to you, so also has the boasting we made to Titus been found to be true. And his affection for you is all the more abundant, as he recalls how obedient you all were and how you received him with fear and trembling. I rejoice that in all things I can have confidence in you.

II. THE COLLECTION FOR THE
POOR CHRISTIANS IN JERUSALEM

Now we make known to you, brethren, the grace of God that has been bestowed upon the churches of Macedonia; where, amid much testing of tribulation, their overflowing joy and their deep poverty have resulted in rich generosity. For according to their means—I bear witness—yes, beyond their means, they gave, earnestly begging of us the favor of sharing in the ministry that is in behalf of the saints. And beyond our expectations they gave themselves, first to the Lord, and then by the will of God to us. This led us to exhort Titus to complete among you also this same gracious work, of which he had made a beginning before.

Now, as you abound in everything—in faith, in utterance, in knowledge, in all zeal, in your love for us—may you excel in this gracious work also. I do not speak as commanding, but as testing the sincerity of your own charity by means of the zeal of others. For you know the graciousness of our Lord Jesus Christ—how, being rich, he became poor for your sakes, that by his poverty you might become rich.

In this matter I am giving advice. It is to your interest, since a year ago you not only began to do, but also to have the will. Now therefore complete the doing also; so that your readiness to begin it may be equaled by your desire to carry it through, according to your ability. For if there is willingness, it is welcome according to what one has, not according to what one does not have.

For I do not mean that the relief of others should become your burden, but that there should be equality; that at the present time your abundance may supply their want, and that their abundance may, in its turn, make up what you lack, thus establishing an equality, as it is written, "He who had much had nothing over, and he who had little had not less."

Now thanks be to God, who has inspired Titus with this same zeal for you. For not only has he accepted our exhortation, but being very zealous himself, he has gone to you of his own choice. And we have sent along with him the brother whose services to the gospel are praised in all the churches; and what is more, who was also appointed by the churches to travel with us in this work of grace which is being done by us, to the glory of the Lord and to show our own readiness. We are on our guard, lest anyone should slander us in the matter of our administration of this generous amount. For we take forethought for what is honorable, not only before God, but also in the sight of men. And we have sent with them also our brother, whom we have proved to be zealous often and in many things, but who now is more in earnest than ever, because of his great confidence in you, whether as regards Titus, who is my companion and fellow-worker among you, or as regards our brethren, the messengers of the churches, the glory of Christ. Give them therefore, in the sight of the churches, a proof of your charity and of our boasting on your behalf.

For it is indeed superfluous for me to write to you with reference to this charitable service to the saints. For I know your eagerness, whereof I boast about you to the Macedonians—that Achaia has been ready since last year—and your zeal has stimulated very many. Still, I have sent the brethren, lest our boasting concerning you should be found empty in this instance; that, as I was saying, you may be ready, lest, if any Macedonians come with me and find you unprepared, we—not to say yourselves—should be put to shame for having been so sure. I have therefore thought it necessary to exhort the brethren to go to you in advance and to get ready this promised contribution, so that it may be as a matter of bounty, not of extortion.

Mark this: he who sows sparingly will also reap sparingly, and he who sows bountifully will also reap bountifully. Let each one give according as he has determined in his heart, not grudgingly or from compulsion, for "God loves a cheerful giver." And God is able to make all grace abound in you, so that always having ample means, you may abound in every good work, as it is written, "He has scattered abroad and has given to the poor, his justice remains forever."

Now he who provides the sower with seed will both give you bread to eat and will multiply your seed, and will increase the growth of the fruits of your justice; that, being enriched in all things, you may contribute with simplicity of purpose, and thus through us evoke thanksgiving to God; for the administration of this service not only supplies the want of the saints, but overflows also in much gratitude to the Lord. The evidence furnished by this service makes them glorify God for your obedient profession of Christ's gospel and for the sincere generosity of your contributions to them and to all; while they themselves, in their prayers for you, yearn for you, because of the excellent grace God has given you. Thanks be to God for his unspeakable gift!

III. THE APOSTLE DEFENDS HIS APOSTOLATE

Now I myself, Paul, appeal to you by the meekness and gentleness of Christ—I who to your face indeed am diffident when among you, but when absent am fearless towards you! Yes, I beseech you that I may not when I come have to be bold, with that assurance wherewith I am thought to be bold, against those who regard us as walking according to the flesh. For though we walk in the flesh, we do not make war according to the flesh; for the weapons of our warfare are not carnal, but powerful before God to the demolishing of strongholds, the destroying of reasoning—yes, of every lofty thing that exalts itself against the knowledge of God, bringing every mind into captivity to the obedience of Christ, and being prepared to take vengeance on all disobedience when once your own submission is complete.

Look at what is before you. If anyone is confident that he is Christ's, let him reflect within himself that even as he is Christ's, so too are we. For even if I boast somewhat more about our authority (which the Lord has given for your upbuilding, and not for your destruction), I shall not be put to shame. But that I may not seem to terrify you, as it were, by letters ("for his letters," they say, "are weighty and telling, but his bodily appearance is weak and his speech of no account"), let such people understand that what we are in word by letter when absent, such are we also in deed when bodily present.

Of course we have not the boldness to class ourselves or to compare ourselves with certain ones who commend themselves. We, on the contrary, measure ourselves by ourselves and compare ourselves with ourselves; and so we do not boast beyond our limits, but within the limits of the commission which God has given us—limits which include you also. For we are not going beyond our commission, as if it did not embrace you, since we reached even as far as you with the gospel of Christ.

We do not boast beyond our limits, in the labors of other men; but we hope, as your faith increases, greatly to enlarge through you the province allotted to us, so as even to preach the gospel in places that lie beyond you, instead of boasting in another man's sphere about work already done. "But he who boasts, let him boast in the Lord." For he is not approved who commends himself, but he whom the Lord commends.

Would to God that you could bear with a little of my foolishness! Nay, do bear with me! For I am jealous for you with a divine jealousy. For I betrothed you to one spouse, that I might present you a chaste virgin to Christ. But I fear lest, as the serpent seduced Eve by his guile, so your minds may be corrupted and fall from a single devotion to Christ. For if he who comes preaches another Christ whom we did not preach, or if you receive another Spirit whom you have not received, or another gospel which you did not accept, you might well bear with him. For I regard myself as nowise inferior to the great apostles. Even though I be rude in speech, yet I am not so in knowledge; but in every way we have made ourselves clear to you.

Or did I do wrong when I humbled myself that you might be exalted, preaching to you the gospel of God free of charge? I stripped other churches, taking pay from them so as to minister to you. And when I was with you and in want, I was a burden to no one; for the brethren from Macedonia supplied my needs. Thus in all things I have kept myself from being a burden to you, and so I intend to keep myself. By the truth of Christ which is in me, this boast shall not be taken from me in the districts of Achaia. Why so? Because I do not love you? God knows I do. But what I do I will go on doing, that I may deprive them of the occasion who are seeking an occasion to boast that they are doing the same as we do. For they are false apostles, deceitful workers, disguising themselves as apostles of Christ. And no wonder, for Satan himself disguises himself as an angel of light. It is no great thing, then, if his ministers disguise themselves as ministers of justice. But their end will be according to their works.

I repeat, let no one think me foolish. But if so, then regard me as such, that I also may boast a little. What I am saying in this confidence of boasting, I am not speaking according to the Lord, but as it were in foolishness. Since many boast according to the flesh, I too will boast. For you gladly put up with fools, because you are wise yourselves! For you suffer it if a man enslaves you, if a man devours you, if a man takes from you, if a man is arrogant, if a man slaps your face! I speak to my own shame, as though we had been weak. But wherein any is bold—I am speaking foolishly—I also am bold. Are they Hebrews? So am I! Are they Israelites? So am I! Are they offspring of Abraham? So am I! Are they ministers of Christ? I—to speak as a fool—am more: in many more labors, in prisons more frequently, in lashes above measure, often exposed to death. From the Jews five times I received forty lashes less one. Thrice I was scourged, once I was stoned, thrice I suffered shipwreck, a night and a day I was adrift on the sea; in journeyings often, in perils from floods, in perils from robbers, in perils from my own nation, in perils from the Gentiles, in perils in the city, in perils in the wilderness, in perils in the sea, in perils from false brethren; in labor and hardships, in many sleepless nights, in hunger and thirst, in fastings often, in cold and nakedness. Besides those outer things, there is my daily pressing anxiety, the care of all the churches! Who is weak, am I not weak? Who is made to stumble, and I am not inflamed? If I must boast, I will boast of the things that concern my weakness.

The God and Father of the Lord Jesus, who is blessed forevermore, knows that I do not lie. In Damascus the governor under King Aretas was guarding the city of the Damascenes in order to arrest me, but I was lowered in a basket through a window in the wall, and escaped his hands.

If I must boast—it is not indeed expedient to do so—but I will come to visions and revelations of the Lord. I know a man in Christ who fourteen years ago—whether in the body I do not know, or out of the body I do not know, God knows—such a one was caught up to the third heaven. And I know such a man—whether in the body or out of the body I do not know, God knows—that he was caught up into paradise and heard secret words that man may not repeat. Of such a man I will boast; but of myself I will glory in nothing save in my infirmities. For if I do wish to boast, I shall not be foolish; for I shall be speaking the truth. But I forbear, lest any man should reckon me beyond what he sees in me or hears from me.

And lest the greatness of the revelations should puff me up, there was given me a thorn for the flesh, a messenger of Satan, to buffet me. Concerning this I thrice besought the Lord that it might leave me. And he has said to me, "My grace is sufficient for thee, for strength is made perfect in weakness." Gladly therefore I will glory in my infirmities, that the strength of Christ may dwell in me. Wherefore I am satisfied, for Christ's sake, with infirmities, with insults, with hardships, with persecutions, with distresses. For when I am weak, then I am strong.

I have become foolish! You have forced me. For I ought to have been commended by you, since in no way have I fallen short of the most eminent apostles, even though I am nothing. Indeed, the signs of the apostle were wrought among you in all patience, in miracles and wonders and deeds of power. For in what have you been less favored than the other churches—unless in this, that I was no burden to you? Pardon me this wrong!

Behold, this is the third time that I am ready to come to you. And I will not be a burden to you; for I do not seek yours, but you. For the children should not save up for the parents, but the parents for the children. But I will most gladly spend and be spent myself for your souls, even though, loving you more, I be loved less.

But be it so: I was no burden to you, but, being crafty, I caught you by guile. Did I take advantage of you through any of these whom I sent to you? I urged Titus to go, and I sent our brother with him. Did Titus take advantage of you? Have we not walked in the same spirit, have we not walked in the same steps?

Are you thinking all this time that we are defending ourselves before you? We speak before God in Christ; but in all things, beloved, for your own edification. For I fear lest perhaps when I come I may not find you as I should wish, and lest I may be found by you not as you would wish—lest perhaps there be found among you contentions, envyings, animosities, dissensions, detractions, gossiping, arrogance, disorders—lest when I come again God should humiliate me before you, and I should mourn over many who sinned before and have not repented of the uncleanness and immorality and licentiousness that they practiced.

Behold, this is the third time that I am coming to you: "On the word of two or three witnesses every word shall be confirmed." I have already warned, when present, and now in my absence I warn again those who sinned before, and all the rest, that, if I come again, I will not spare. Do you seek a proof of the Christ who speaks in me, who is not weak in your regard, nay, is powerful in you? For though he was crucified through weakness, yet he lives through the power of God. Yes, we also are weak in him, yet we shall live with him through the power of God in your regard.

Put your own selves to test, whether you are in the faith; prove yourselves. Do you not know yourselves that Christ Jesus is in you? unless perhaps you are reprobate! But I hope that you will come to know that we are not reprobate. But we pray God that you may do no evil at all, not wishing ourselves to appear approved, but that you may do what is good, and we ourselves pass as reprobate. For we can do nothing against the truth, but only for the truth. And so we rejoice when we are weak but you are strong. This we also pray for, your perfecting.

Wherefore I write these things while absent, that when present I may not act more severely, according to the power that the Lord has given me for upbuilding, and not for destruction.

CONCLUSION

In conclusion, brethren, rejoice, be perfected, be comforted, be of the same mind, be at peace; and the God of peace and love will be with you. Greet one another with a holy kiss. All the saints send you greetings.

The grace of our Lord Jesus Christ, and the charity of God, and the fellowship of the Holy Spirit be with you all. Amen.

A Note about
The Epistle of St. Paul the Apostle
to the Galatians

The Galatians to whom this Epistle was written were Gentile Christians and were converted by St. Paul about the year A.D. 52. His ministry among them had borne great fruit; they had been baptized and had received the Holy Spirit; miracles worked among them had given evidence of the presence of the Spirit in their hearts. The Apostle visited them a second time, and by his exhortations confirmed them in the faith. But after his second visit St. Paul learned, by letter or by special messenger sent to him, that some Jewish teachers who had lately arrived among his new converts were teaching, contrary to his doctrines, that for salvation it was necessary to be circumcised and to observe the Mosaic rites. Furthermore, these Judaizers sought to undermine the authority of the Apostle by questioning his divine commission. They claimed that his teaching seemed to be only human and differed widely in many respects from that of Christ and of the other Apostles. They asserted that he disregarded the sacredness of the Mosaic Law and circumcision, which were an external sign of God's covenant with man, and thereby doubted the truth of the divine promises. Such were the difficulties that reached the ears of St. Paul in Ephesus; and since he was unable to be with his converts, he met the serious situation by this Epistle.

The Epistle contains a defense of his person and of his doctrine. In indignation he asserts the divine origin of his teaching and of his authority; he shows that justification is not through the Mosaic Law, but through faith in Jesus Christ, who was crucified and who rose from the dead; he concludes that consequently the Mosaic Law was not permanent, that it is not an essential part of Christianity.

The subject matter of the Epistle resembles closely that of the Epistle to the Romans and also of the Second Epistle to the Corinthians. The reason for this similarity is that these Epistles were written when the Apostle was more or less in the same frame of mind, indignant that his converts were being perverted by Pharisaic emissaries.

The Epistle of St. Paul the Apostle
to the Galatians

INTRODUCTION

Paul, an apostle, sent not from men nor by man, but by Jesus
Christ and God the Father who raised him from the dead,
and all the brethren who are with me, to the churches of
Galatia. Grace and peace be to you from God the Father,
and from our Lord Jesus Christ, who gave himself for our
sins, that he might deliver us from the wickedness of this
present world according to the will of our God and Father;
to whom is glory forever and ever. Amen.

I marvel that you are so quickly deserting him who
called you to the grace of Christ, changing to another gospel; which is not another gospel, except in this respect that
there are some who trouble you, and wish to pervert the
gospel of Christ. But even if we or an angel from heaven
should preach a gospel to you other than that which we
have preached to you, let him be anathema! As we have
said before, so now I say again: If anyone preach a gospel
to you other than that which you have received, let him be
anathema! For am I now seeking the favor of men, or of

God? Or am I seeking to please men? If I were still trying to please men, I should not be a servant of Christ.

I. PERSONAL DEFENSE

For I give you to understand, brethren, that the gospel which was preached by me is not of man. For I did not receive it from man, nor was I taught it; but I received it by a revelation of Jesus Christ. For you have heard of my former manner of life in Judaism; how beyond all measure I persecuted the Church of God, and ravaged it. And I advance in Judaism above many of my contemporaries in my nation, showing much more zeal for the traditions of my fathers. But when it pleased him who from my mother's womb set me apart and called me by his grace, to reveal his Son in me, that I might preach him among the Gentiles, immediately, without taking counsel with flesh and blood, and without going up to Jerusalem to those who were appointed apostles before me, I retired into Arabia, and again returned to Damascus.

Then after three years I went to Jerusalem to see Peter, and I remained with him fifteen days. But I saw none of the other apostles, except James, the brother of the Lord. Now in what I am writing to you, behold, before God, I do not lie. Then I went into the regions of Syria and Cilicia. And I was unknown by sight to the churches of Judea which were in Christ. But they had heard only that he who formerly persecuted us, now preaches the faith which once he ravaged. And they glorified God in me.

Then after fourteen years I went up again to Jerusalem with Barnabas, taking also Titus along with me. And I went up in consequence of a revelation, and I conferred with them on the gospel which I preach among the Gentiles, but separately with the men of authority; lest perhaps I should be running, or had run in vain. But not even Titus, who was with me, Gentile though he was, was compelled to be circumcised, although it was urged on account of false brethren who were brought in secretly, who slipped in to spy upon our liberty which we have in Christ Jesus, that they might bring us into slavery. Now to these we did not yield in submission, no, not for an hour, that the truth of the gospel might continue with you. But from the men of authority (what they once were matters not to me; God accepts not the person of man)—the men of authority laid no further burden on me. On the contrary, when they saw that to me was committed the gospel for the uncircumcised, as to Peter that for the circumcised (for he who worked in Peter for the apostleship of the circumcised worked also in me among the Gentiles)—and when they recognized the grace that was given to me, James and Cephas and John, who were considered the pillars, gave to me and to Barnabas the right hand of fellowship, that we should go to the Gentiles, and they to the circumcised; provided only that we should be mindful of the poor, the very thing I was eager to do.

But when Cephas came to Antioch, I withstood him to his face, because he was deserving of blame. For before certain persons came from James, he used to eat with the Gentiles; but when they came, he began to withdraw and to separate himself, fearing the circumcised. And the rest of the Jews dissembled along with him, so that Barnabas also was led away by them into that dissimulation. But when I saw that they were not walking uprightly according to the truth of the gospel, I said to Cephas before them all: If thou, though a Jew, livest like the Gentiles, and not like the Jews, how is it that thou dost compel the Gentiles to live like the Jews?

We are Jews by birth, and not sinners from among the Gentiles. But we know that man is not justified by the works of the Law, but by the faith of Jesus Christ. Hence we also believe in Christ Jesus, that we may be justified by the faith of Christ, and not by the works of the Law; because by the works of the Law no man will be justified. But if, while we are seeking to be justified in Christ, we ourselves also are found sinners, is Christ therefore the minister of sin? By no means. For if I reconstruct the things that I destroyed, I make myself a sinner. For I through the Law have died to the Law that I may live to God. With Christ I am nailed to the cross. It is now no longer I that live, but Christ lives in me. And the life that I now live in the flesh, I live in the faith of the Son of God, who loved me and gave himself up for me. I do not cast away the grace of God. For if justice is by the Law, then Christ died in vain.

II. DOCTRINAL

O foolish Galatians! Who has bewitched you, before whose eyes Jesus Christ has been depicted crucified? This only I would learn from you: Did you receive the Spirit in virtue of the works of the Law, or in virtue of hearing and believing? Are you so foolish that after beginning in the Spirit, you now make a finish in the flesh? Have you suffered so much in vain? if indeed it was in vain. He therefore who gives the Spirit to you, and works miracles among you, does he do it by the works of the Law, or by the message of faith? Even thus "Abraham believed God, and it was credited to him as justice."

Know therefore that the men of faith are the real sons of Abraham. And the Scripture, foreseeing that God would justify the Gentiles by faith, announced to Abraham beforehand, "In thee shall all the nations be blessed." Therefore the men of faith shall be blessed with faithful Abraham.

For those who rely on the works of the Law are under a curse. For it is written, "Cursed is everyone who does not hold to all things that are written in the book of the Law, to perform them." But that by the Law no man is justified before God is evident, because "he who is just lives by faith." But the Law does not rest on faith; but, "he who does these things, shall live by them." Christ redeemed us from the curse of the Law, becoming a curse for us; for it is written, "Cursed is everyone who hangs on a gibbet"; that the blessing of Abraham might come to the Gentiles through Christ Jesus, that through faith we might receive the promise of the Spirit.

Brethren (I speak after the manner of men); yet even a man's will, once it has been ratified, no one annuls or alters. The promises were made to Abraham and to his offspring. He does not say, "And to his offsprings," as of many; but as of one, "And to thy offspring," who is Christ. Now I mean this: The Law which was made four hundred and thirty years later does not annul the covenant which was ratified by God, so as to make the promise void. For if the right to inherit be from the Law, it is no longer from a promise. But God gave it to Abraham by promise.

What then was the Law? It was enacted on account of transgressions, being delivered by angels through a mediator, until the offspring should come to whom the promise was made. Now there is no intermediary where there is only one; but God is one. Is the Law then contrary to the promises of God? By no means. For if a law had been given that could give life, justice would truly be from the Law. But the Scripture shut up all things under sin, that by the faith of Jesus Christ the promise might be given to those who believe.

But before the faith came we were kept imprisoned under the Law, shut up for the faith that was to be revealed. Therefore the Law has been our tutor unto Christ, that we might be justified by faith. But now that faith has come, we are no longer under a tutor. For you are all the children of God through faith in Christ Jesus. For all you who have been baptized into Christ, have put on Christ. There is neither Jew nor Greek; there is neither slave nor freeman; there is neither male nor female. For you are all one in Christ Jesus. And if you are Christ's, then you are the offspring of Abraham, heirs according to promise.

Now I say, as long as the heir is a child, he differs in no way from a slave, though he is the master of all; but he is under guardians and stewards until the time set by his father. So we too, when we were children, were enslaved under the elements of the world. But when the fullness of time came, God sent his Son, born of a woman, born under the Law, that he might redeem those who were under the Law, that we might receive the adoption of sons. And because you are sons, God has sent the Spirit of his Son into our hearts, crying, "Abba, Father." So that he is no longer a slave, but a son; and if a son, an heir also through God.

But then indeed, not knowing God, you served those who really are not gods. But now that you have come to know God, or rather to be known by God, how is it that you turn again to the weak and beggarly elements, which you desire to serve again? You are observing days and months and seasons and years. I fear for you, lest perhaps I have labored among you in vain.

Become like me, because I also have become like you, brethren, I beseech you! You have done me no wrong. And you know that on account of a physical infirmity I preached the gospel to you formerly; and though I was a trial to you in my flesh, you did not reject or despise me; but you received me as an angel of God, even as Christ Jesus. Where then is your self-congratulation? For I bear you witness that, if possible, you would have plucked out your very eyes and given them to me. Have I then become your enemy, because I tell you the truth? They court you from no good motive; but they would estrange you, that you may court them. But court the good from a good motive always, and not only when I am present with you, my dear children, with whom I am in labor again, until Christ is formed in you! But I wish I could be with you now, and change my tone, because I do not know what to make of you.

Tell me, you who desire to be under the Law, have you not read the Law? For it is written that Abraham had two sons, the one by a slave-girl and the other by a free woman. And the son of the slave-girl was born according to the flesh, but the son of the free woman in virtue of the promise. This is said by way of allegory. For these are the two covenants: one indeed from Mount Sinai, bringing forth children unto bondage, which is Agar. For Sinai is a mountain in Arabia, which corresponds to the present Jerusalem, and is in slavery with her children. But that Jerusalem which is above is free, which is our mother. For it is written, "Rejoice thou barren, that dost not bear; break forth and cry, thou that dost not travail; for many are the children of the desolate, more than of her that has a husband." Now we, brethren, are the children of promise, as Isaac was. But as then he who was born according to the flesh persecuted him who was born according to the spirit, so also it is now. But what does the Scripture say? "Cast out the slave-girl and her son, for the son of the slave-girl shall not be heir with the son of the free woman." Therefore, brethren, we are not children of a slave-girl, but of the free woman—in virtue of the freedom wherewith Christ has made us free.

III. MORAL

Stand fast, and do not be caught again under the yoke of slavery. Behold, I, Paul, tell you that if you be circumcised, Christ will be of no advantage to you. And I testify again to every man who has himself circumcised, that he is bound to observe the whole Law. You who would be justified in the Law are estranged from Christ; you have fallen away from grace. For we in the Spirit wait for the hope of justice in virtue of faith. For in Christ Jesus neither circumcision is of any avail, nor uncircumcision, but faith which works through charity.

You were running well; who hindered you from obeying the truth? This persuasion is not from him who calls you. A little leaven ferments the whole mass. I have confidence in you in the Lord, that you will not think otherwise; but he who disturbs you will bear the penalty, whoever he may be. But I, brethren, if I still preach circumcision, why am I still persecuted? Then the stumbling-block of the cross is removed! Would that those who are unsettling you would mutilate themselves!

For you have been called to liberty, brethren; only do not use liberty as an occasion for sensuality, but by charity serve one another. For the whole Law is fulfilled in one word: Thou shalt love thy neighbor as thyself. But if you bite and devour one another, take heed or you will be consumed by one another.

But I say: Walk in the Spirit, and you will not fulfill the lusts of the flesh. For the flesh lusts against the spirit, and the spirit against the flesh; for these are opposed to each other, so that you do not do what you would. But if you are led by the Spirit, you are not under the Law. Now the works of the flesh are manifest, which are immorality, uncleanness, licentiousness, idolatry, witchcrafts, enmities, contentions, jealousies, anger, quarrels, factions, parties, envies, murders, drunkenness, carousings, and suchlike. And concerning these I warn you, as I have warned you, that they who do such things will not attain the kingdom of God. But the fruit of the Spirit is: charity, joy, peace, patience, kindness, goodness, faith, modesty, continency. Against such things there is no law. And they who belong to Christ have crucified their flesh with its passions and desires. If we live by the Spirit, by the Spirit let us also walk. Let us not become desirous of vainglory, provoking one another, envying one another.

Brethren, even if a person is caught doing something wrong, you who are spiritual instruct such a one in a spirit of meekness, considering thyself, lest thou also be tempted. Bear one another's burdens, and so you will fulfill the law of Christ. For if anyone thinks himself to be something, whereas he is nothing, he deceives himself. But let everyone test his own work, and so he will have glory in himself only, and not in comparison with another. For each one will bear his own burden.

And let him who is instructed in the word share all good things with his teacher. Be not deceived, God is not mocked. For what a man sows, that he will also reap. For he who sows in the flesh, from the flesh also will reap corruption. But he who sows in the spirit, from the spirit will reap life everlasting. And in doing good let us not grow tired; for in due time, let us do good to all men, but especially to those who are of the household of faith.

CONCLUSION

See with what large letters I am writing to you with my own hand! As many as wish to please in the flesh compel you to be circumcised simply that they may not suffer persecution for the cross of Christ. For not even they who are circumcised keep the Law; but they desire you to be circumcised, that they may make a boast of your flesh. But as for me, God forbid that I should glory save in the cross of our Lord Jesus Christ, through whom the world is crucified to me, and I to the world. For in Christ Jesus neither circumcision nor uncircumcision but a new creation is of any account.

And whoever follow this rule, peace and mercy upon them, even unto the Israel of God.

Henceforth let no man give me trouble, for I bear the marks of the Lord Jesus in my body. The grace of our Lord Jesus Christ be with your spirit, brethren. Amen.

A Note *about*
The Epistle of St. Paul the Apostle
to the Ephesians

This Epistle was written by St. Paul towards the close of his first imprisonment in Rome, in the year A.D. 63.

In spite of this traditional title it is uncertain to whom St. Paul originally addressed this Epistle. Either it was indeed written to the Ephesians, as was commonly believed from the end of the second century A.D. and indicated by the presence of the words "at Ephesus" (1:1) in most manuscripts; or it is to be identified with the Epistle mentioned in Colossians 4:16, which St. Paul wrote to the Christians of Laodicea, a town not far from Colossae and Ephesus; or, finally, it may have been written, not to any one community in particular, but as a sort of circular letter to the various Christian communities in that part of Asia Minor in which Ephesus and Colossae are situated.

Ephesus, then the chief city of western Asia Minor, had been evangelized by St. Paul about A.D. 53–56. Soon afterwards the important town of Laodicea, about a hundred miles to the east, had received Christianity from some Ephesian Christians. The great majority of converts in all this

territory were from among the pagan Gentiles, Jews forming
only a small minority.

Very similar in theme and language to the Epistle to the
Colossians, but much more abstract, profound, and system-
atic, this Epistle's central thought is the Church regarded as
the mystical body of Christ, through which God pours out
the divine life of grace in most generous fashion to its members, the Christians, in and through its head, Jesus Christ.
The spiritual, organic unity of its members with Christ and
with one another is emphasized as the basic principle of the
life of the mystical body. Then comes exhortations to lead
the new life that befits those incorporated into the sublime
unity of the mystical body.

The Epistle of St. Paul the Apostle
to the Ephesians

INTRODUCTION

Paul, an apostle of Jesus Christ by the will of God, to all the saints who are at Ephesus, the faithful in Christ Jesus: grace be to you and peace from God our Father and the Lord Jesus Christ.

Blessed be the God and Father of our Lord Jesus Christ, who has blessed us with every spiritual blessing on high in Christ. Even as he chose us in him before the foundation of the world, that we should be holy and without blemish in his sight in love. He predestined us to be adopted through Jesus Christ as his sons, according to the purpose of his will, unto the praise of the glory of his grace, with which he has favored us in his beloved Son.

In him we have redemption through his blood, the remission of sins, according to the riches of his grace. This grace has abounded beyond measure in us in all wisdom and prudence, so that he may make known to us the mystery of his will according to his good pleasure. And this his good pleasure he purposed in him to be dispensed in the fullness of the times: to re-establish all things in Christ, both those in the heavens and those on the earth.

In him, I say, in whom we also have been called by a special choice, having been predestined in the purpose of him who works all things according to the counsel of his will, to contribute to the praise of his glory—we who before hoped in Christ. And in him you too, when you had heard the word of truth, the good news of your salvation, and believed in it, were sealed with the Holy Spirit of the promise, who is the pledge of our inheritance, for a redemption of possession, for the praise of his glory.

I. DOCTRINAL

Wherefore I on my part, hearing of your faith in the Lord Jesus, and of your love for all the saints, do not cease to give thanks for you, making mention of you in my prayers, that the God of our Lord Jesus Christ, the Father of glory, may grant you the spirit of wisdom and revelation in deep knowledge of him: the eyes of your mind being enlightened, so that you may know what is the hope of his calling, what the riches of the glory of his inheritance in the saints, and what the exceeding greatness of his power towards us who believe.

Its measure is the working of his mighty power, which he has wrought in Christ in raising him from the dead, and setting him at his right hand in heaven above every Principality and Power and Virtue and Domination—in short, above every name that is named, not only in this world, but also in that which is to come. And all things he made subject under his feet, and him he gave as head over all the Church, which indeed is his body, the completion of him who fills all with all.

You also, when you were dead by reason of your offenses and sins, wherein once you walked according to the fashion of this world, according to the prince of the power of the air about us, the prince of the spirit which now works on the unbelievers—indeed, in the company of these even we, all of us, once led our lives in the desires of our flesh, doing the promptings of our flesh and of our thoughts, and were by nature children of wrath even as the rest. But God, who is rich in mercy, by reason of his very great love wherewith he has loved us even when we were dead by reason of our sins, brought us to life together with Christ (by grace you have been saved), and raised us up together, and seated us together in heaven in Christ Jesus, that he might show in the ages to come the overflowing riches of his grace in kindness towards us in Christ Jesus. For by grace you have been saved through faith; and that not from yourselves, for it is the gift of God; not as the outcome of works, lest anyone may boast. For his workmanship we are, created in Christ Jesus in good works, which God has made ready beforehand that we may walk in them.

Wherefore, bear in mind that once you, the Gentiles in flesh, who are called "uncircumcision" by the so-called "circumcision" in flesh made by human hand—bear in mind that you were at that time without Christ, excluded as aliens from the community of Israel, and strangers to the covenants of the promise; having no hope, and without God in the world. But now in Christ Jesus you, who were once afar off, have been brought near through the blood of Christ.

For he himself is our peace, he it is who has made both one, and has broken down the intervening wall of the enclosure, the enmity, in his flesh. The Law of the commandments expressed in decrees he has made void, that of the two he might create in himself one new man, and make peace and reconcile both in one body to God by the cross, having slain the enmity in himself. And coming, he announced the good tidings of peace to you who were afar off, and of peace to those who were near; because through him we both have access in one Spirit to the Father. Therefore, you are now no longer strangers and foreigners, but you are citizens with the saints and members of God's household: you are built upon the foundation of the apostles and prophets with Christ Jesus himself as the chief corner stone. In him the whole structure is closely fitted together and grows into a temple holy in the Lord; in him you too are being built together into a dwelling place for God in the Spirit.

For this reason, I, Paul, the prisoner of Christ Jesus for the sake of you, the Gentiles—for I suppose you have heard of the dispensation of the grace of God that was given to me in your regard; how that by revelation was made known to me the mystery, as I have written above in brief; and so by reading you can perceive how well versed I am in the mystery of Christ, that mystery which in other ages was not known to the sons of men, as now it has been revealed to his holy apostles and prophets in the Spirit: namely, that the Gentiles are joint heirs, and fellow-members of the same body, and joint partakers of the promise in Christ Jesus through the gospel.

Of that gospel I was made a minister by the gift of God's grace, which was given to me in accordance with the working of his power. Yes, to me, the very least of all saints, there was given this grace, to announce among the Gentiles the good tidings of the unfathomable riches of Christ, and to enlighten all man as to what is the dispensation of the mystery which has been hidden from eternity in God, who created all things; in order that through the Church there be made known to the Principalities and the Powers in the heavens the manifold wisdom of God according to the eternal purpose which he accomplished in Christ Jesus our Lord. In him we have assurance and confident access through faith in him. Therefore I pray you not to be disheartened at my tribulations for you, for they are your glory.

For this reason I bend my knees to the Father of our Lord Jesus Christ, from whom all fatherhood in heaven and on earth receives its name, that he may grant you from his glorious riches to be strengthened with power through his Spirit unto the progress of the inner man; and to have Christ dwelling through faith in your hearts: so that, being rooted and grounded in love, you may be able to comprehend with all the saints what is the breadth and length and height and depth, and to know Christ's love which surpasses knowledge, in order that you may be filled unto all the fullness of God.

Now, to him who is able to accomplish all things in a measure far beyond what we ask or conceive, in keeping with the power that is at work in us—to him be glory in the Church and in Christ Jesus down through all the ages of time without end. Amen.

II. MORAL

I therefore, the prisoner in the Lord, exhort you to walk in a manner worthy of the calling with which you were called, with all humility and meekness, with patience, bearing with one another in love, careful to preserve the unity of the Spirit in the bond of peace: one body and one Spirit, even as you were called in one hope of your calling; one Lord, one faith, one Baptism; one God and Father of all, who is above all, and throughout all, and in us all.

But to each one of us grace was given according to the measure of Christ's bestowal. Thus it says, "Ascending on high, he led away captives; he gave gifts to men." Now this, "he ascended," what does it mean but that he also first descended into the lower parts of the earth? He who descended, he it is who ascended also above all the heavens, that he might fill all things. And he himself gave some men as apostles, and some as prophets, others again as evangelists, and others as pastors and teachers, in order to perfect the saints for a work of ministry, for building up the body of Christ, until we all attain to the unity of the faith and of the deep knowledge of the Son of God, to perfect manhood, to the mature measure of the fullness of Christ. And this he has done that we may be now no longer children, tossed to and fro and carried about by every wind of doctrine devised in the wickedness of men, in craftiness, according to the wiles of error. Rather are we to practice the truth in love, and so grow up in all things in him who is the head, Christ. For from him the whole body (being closely joined and knit together through every joint of the system according to the functioning in due measure of each single part) derives its increase to the building up of itself in love.

This, therefore, I say and testify in the Lord, that henceforward you are not to walk as the Gentiles walk in the futility of their mind, having their understanding clouded in darkness, estranged from the life of God through the ignorance that is in them, because of the blindness of their heart. For they have given themselves up in despair to sensuality, greedily practising every kind of uncleanness. But you have not so learned Christ—for surely you have heard of him and have been taught in him (as truth is in Jesus) that as regards your former manner of life you are to put off the old man, which is being corrupted through its deceptive lusts. But be renewed in the spirit of your mind, and put on the new man, which has been created according to God in justice and holiness of truth.

Wherefore, put away lying and speak truth each one with his neighbor, because we are members of one another. "Be angry and do not sin": do not let the sun go down upon your anger: do not give place to the devil. He who was wont to steal, let him steal no longer; but rather let him labor, working with his hands at what is good, that he may have something to share with him who suffers need. Let no ill speech proceed from your mouth, but whatever is good for supplying what fits the current necessity, that it may give grace to the hearers. And do not grieve the Holy Spirit of God, in whom you were sealed for the day of redemption. Let all bitterness, and wrath, and indignation, and clamor, and reviling, be removed from you, along with all malice. On the contrary, be kind to one another, and merciful, generously forgiving one another, as also God in Christ has generously forgiven you.

Be you, therefore, imitators of God, as very dear children and walk in love, as Christ also loved us and delivered himself up for us an offering and a sacrifice to God to ascend in fragrant odor.

But immorality and every uncleanness or covetousness, let it not even be named among you, as becomes saints; or obscenity or foolish talk or scurrility, which are out of place; but rather thanksgiving. For know this and understand, that no fornicator, or unclean person, or covetous one (for that is idolatry) has any inheritance in the kingdom of Christ and God. Let no one lead you astray with empty words; for because of these things the wrath of God comes upon the children of disobedience. Do not, then, become partakers with them. For you were once darkness, but now you are light in the Lord. Walk, then, as children of light (for the fruit of the light is in all goodness and justice and truth), testing what is well pleasing to God; and have no fellowship with the unfruitful works of darkness, but rather expose them. For of the things that are done by them in secret it is shameful even to speak; but all the things that are exposed are made manifest by the light: for all that is made manifest is light. Thus it says, "Awake, sleeper, and arise from among the dead, and Christ will enlighten thee." See to it therefore, brethren, that you walk with care: not as unwise but as wise, making the most of your time, because the days are evil. Therefore do not become foolish, but understand what the will of the Lord is. And do not be drunk with wine, for in that is debauchery; but be filled with the Spirit, speaking to one another in psalms and hymns and spiritual songs, singing and making melody in your hearts to the Lord, giving thanks always for all things in the name of our Lord Jesus Christ to God the Father.

Be subject to one another in the fear of Christ. Let wives be subject to their husbands as to the Lord; because a husband is head of the wife, just as Christ is head of the Church, being himself savior of the body. But just as the Church is subject to Christ, so also let wives be to their husbands in all things.

Husbands, love your wives, just as Christ also loved the Church, and delivered himself up for her, that he might sanctify her, cleansing her in the bath of water by means of the word; in order that he might present to himself the Church in all her glory, not having spot or wrinkle or any such thing, but that she might be holy and without blemish. Even thus ought husbands also to love their wives as their own bodies. He who loves his own wife, loves himself. For no one ever hated his own flesh; on the contrary he nourishes and cherishes it, as Christ also does the Church (because we are members of his body, made from his flesh and from his bones). "For this cause a man shall leave his father and mother, and cleave to his wife; and the two shall become one flesh." This is a great mystery—I mean in reference to Christ and to the Church. However, let each one of you also love his wife just as he loves himself; and let the wife respect her husband.

Children, obey your parents in the Lord, for that is right. "Honor thy father and thy mother"—such is the first commandment with a promise—"that it may be well with thee, and that thou mayest be long-lived upon the earth."

And you, fathers, do not provoke your children to anger, but rear them in the discipline and admonition of the Lord.

Slaves, obey your masters according to the flesh, with fear and trembling in the sincerity of your heart, as you would Christ: not serving to the eye as pleasers of men, but as slaves of Christ, doing the will of God from your heart, giving your service with good will as to the Lord and not to men, in the knowledge that whatever good each does, the same he will receive back from the Lord, whether he is slave or freeman.

And you, masters, do the same towards them, and give up threatening, knowing that their Lord who is also your Lord is in heaven and that with him there is no respect of persons.

For the rest, brethren, be strengthened in the Lord and in the might of his power. Put on the armor of God, that you may be able to stand against the wiles of the devil. For our wrestling is not against flesh and blood, but against the Principalities and the Powers, against the world-rulers of this darkness, against the spiritual forces of wickedness on high. Therefore take up the armor of God, that you may be able to resist in the evil day, and stand in all things perfect. Stand, therefore, having girded your loins with truth, and having put on the breastplate of justice, and having your feet shod with the readiness of the gospel of peace, in all things taking up the shield of faith, with which you may be able to quench all the fiery darts of the most wicked one. And take unto you the helmet of salvation and the sword of the spirit, that is, the word of God.

With all prayer and supplication pray at all times in the Spirit, and therein be vigilant in all perseverance and supplication for all the saints—and for me, that when I open my mouth, utterance may be granted to me fearlessly to make known the mystery of the gospel, for which I am an ambassador in chains; so that therein I may dare to speak as I ought.

CONCLUSION

But that you too may know my circumstances and what I am doing, Tychicus, our dearest brother and faithful minister in the Lord, will tell you everything. Him have I sent to you for this very purpose, that you may learn our circumstances, and that he may comfort your hearts.

Peace be to the brethren, and love with faith, from God the Father and the Lord Jesus Christ. Grace be with all those who have a love unfailing for our Lord Jesus Christ. Amen.

A Note *about*
The Epistle of St. Paul the Apostle
to the Philippians

The church at Philippi was St. Paul's first foundation on European soil. The vision of a man of Macedonia calling for aid brought the Apostle, St. Timothy, and their comrades from Asia into Europe. In Acts (16:11–40) St. Luke narrates the conversions at Philippi, the cure of a girl possessed by a demon, the Apostle's imprisonment, his release, and his departure from that city.

On at least two other occasions Philippi had the joy of welcoming its beloved Apostle. The people were deeply attached to St. Paul, helping him by alms in his missionary work; and Paul's special affection for them manifests itself in this Epistle. He hopes to be able to visit them soon.

The occasion of its composition can be gathered from the Epistle. Learning that St. Paul had been cast into prison, the church at Philippi, in order to assist him, sent Epaphroditus with a sum of money and with instructions to remain beside the Apostle as his companion and servant. While thus employed, Epaphroditus fell sick and nearly died. Upon his recovery, St. Paul decided to send him back to Philippi.

The Epistle expresses gratitude to the church for its gift and commends the service rendered by Epaphroditus.

At the same time Paul takes the opportunity of exhorting the faithful to compose their dissensions, and he warns them against Jewish converts who wished to make Old Testament practices obligatory for Christians.

No one but St. Paul could have composed such a letter. It was written from Rome in A.D. 63.

The Epistle of St. Paul the Apostle
to the Philippians

INTRODUCTION

Paul and Timothy, servants of Jesus Christ, to all the saints in Christ Jesus that are at Philippi, with the bishops and deacons: grace be to you, and peace from God our Father, and from the Lord Jesus Christ.

I give thanks to my God in all my remembrance of you, always in all my prayers making supplications for you all with joy, because of your association with me in spreading the gospel of Christ from the first day until now. I am convinced of this, that he who has begun a good work in you will bring it to perfection until the day of Christ Jesus. And I have the right to feel so about you all, because I have you in my heart, all of you, alike in my chains and in the defense and confirmation of the gospel, as sharers in my joy. For God is my witness how I long for you all in the heart of Christ Jesus. And this I pray, that your charity may more and more abound in knowledge and all discernment, so that you may approve the better things, that you may be upright and without offense unto the day of Christ, filled with the fruit of justice, through Jesus Christ, to the glory and praise of God.

I. PERSONAL NEWS

Now I wish you to know, brethren, that my experiences have turned out rather for the advancement of the gospel, so that the chains I bear for the sake of Christ have become manifest as such throughout the praetorium and in all other places. And the greater number of the brethren in the Lord, gaining courage from my chains, have dared to speak the word of God more freely and without fear. Some indeed preach Christ even out of envy and contentiousness, but some also out of good will. Some proclaim Christ out of love since they know I am appointed for the defense of the gospel; but some out of contentiousness, not sincerely, thinking to stir up affliction for me in my chains. But what of it? Provided only that in every way, whether in pretense or in truth, Christ is being proclaimed; in this I rejoice, yes and I shall rejoice. For I know that this will turn out for my salvation, thanks to your prayer and the assistance of the Spirit of Jesus Christ, in accord with my eager longing and hope that in nothing I shall be put to shame, but that with complete assurance now as at all times Christ will be glorified in my body, whether through life or through death.

For to me to live is Christ and to die is gain. But if to live in the flesh is my lot, this means for me fruitful labor, and I do not know which to choose. Indeed I am hard pressed from both sides—desiring to depart and to be with Christ, a lot by far the better; yet to stay on in the flesh is necessary for your sake. And with this conviction I know that I shall stay on and continue with you all for your progress and joy in the faith, that your rejoicing in my regard may abound in Christ Jesus through my coming to you again.

II. EXHORTATION

Only let your lives be worthy of the gospel of Christ; so that, whether I come and see you, or remain absent, I may hear about you, that you are steadfast in one spirit, with one mind striving together for the faith of the gospel. Do not be terrified in any way by the adversaries; for this is to them a reason for destruction, but to you for salvation, and that from God. For you have been given the favor on Christ's behalf—not only to believe in him but also to suffer for him, while engaged in the same struggle in which you have seen me and now have heard of me.

If, therefore, there is any comfort in Christ, any encouragement from charity, any fellowship in the Spirit, any feelings of mercy, fill up my joy by thinking alike, having the same charity, with one soul and one mind. Do nothing out of contentiousness or out of vainglory, but in humility let each one regard the others as his superiors, each one looking not to his own interests but to those of others.

Have this mind in you which was also in Christ Jesus, who though he was by nature God, did not consider being equal to God a thing to be clung to, but emptied himself, taking the nature of a slave and being made like unto men. And appearing in the form of a man, he humbled himself, becoming obedient to death, even to death on a cross. Therefore

God also has exalted him and has bestowed upon him the name that is above every name, so that at the name of Jesus every knee should bend of those in heaven, on earth and under the earth, and every tongue should confess that the Lord Jesus Christ is in the glory of God the Father.

Wherefore, my beloved, obedient as you have always been, not as in my presence only, but now much more in my absence, work out your salvation with fear and trembling. For it is God who of his good pleasure works in you both the will and the performance. Do all things without murmuring and without questioning, so as to be blameless and guileless, children of God without blemish in the midst of a depraved and perverse generation. For among these you shine like stars in the world, holding fast the word of life to my glory against the day of Christ; because not in vain have I run, neither in vain have I labored. But even if I am made the libation for the sacrifice and service of your faith, I joy and rejoice with you. And in the same way do you also joy and rejoice with me.

III. TIMOTHY AND EPAPHRODITUS

Now I hope in the Lord Jesus shortly to send Timothy to you, that I also may be of good cheer when I know your circumstances. For I have no one so like-minded who is so genuinely solicitous for you. For they all seek their own interests, not those of Jesus Christ. But know his worth: as child serves father, so he has served with me in spreading the gospel. I hope then to send him to you as soon as I see how things stand with me. But I trust in the Lord that I myself also shall come to you shortly.

But I have thought it necessary to send to you Epaphroditus, my brother and fellow-worker and fellow-soldier, but for you a messenger and the minister to my need. For he was longing for all of you and was grieved because you had heard that he was sick. Yes, he was sick, almost unto death. But God had mercy on him, and not on him only but on me also, that I might not have sorrow upon sorrow. Therefore I send him the more speedily, in order that seeing him again you may rejoice and that I may be free from sorrow. Welcome him, then, with all joy in the Lord and show honor to men like him, because for the work of Christ he drew near to death, risking his life to supply what was lacking for your service to me.

IV. WARNINGS AGAINST FALSE TEACHERS

For the rest, my brethren, rejoice in the Lord. To write you the same things indeed is not irksome to me, but it is necessary for you. Beware of the dogs, beware of the evil workers, beware of the mutilation. For we are the circumcision, we who serve God in spirit, who glory in Christ Jesus and have no confidence in the flesh—though I too might have confidence even in the flesh. If anyone else thinks he may have confidence in the flesh, yet more may I: circumcised the eighth day, of the race of Israel, of the tribe of Benjamin, a Hebrew of Hebrews; as regards the Law, a Pharisee; as regards zeal, a persecutor of the Church of God; as regards the justice of the Law, leading a blameless life.

But the things that were gain to me, these, for the sake of Christ, I have counted loss. Nay more, I count everything loss because of the excelling knowledge of Jesus Christ, my Lord. For his sake I have suffered the loss of all things, and I count them as dung that I may gain Christ and be found in him, not having a justice of my own, which is from the Law, but that which is from faith in Christ, the justice from God based upon faith; so that I may know him and the power of his resurrection and the fellowship of his sufferings: become like to him in death, in the hope that somehow I may attain to the resurrection from the dead. Not that I have already obtained this, or already have been made perfect, but I press on hoping that I may lay hold of that for which Christ Jesus has laid hold of me. Brethren, I do not consider that I have laid hold of it already. But one thing I do: forgetting what is behind, I strain forward to what is before, I press on towards the goal, to the prize of God's heavenly call in Christ Jesus.

Let us then, as many as are perfect, be of this mind; and if in any point you are minded otherwise, this also God will reveal to you. Still in what we have attained let us be of the same mind, and let us also continue in this same rule.

Brethren, be imitators of me, and mark those who work after the pattern you have in us. For many walk, of whom I have told you often and now tell you even weeping, that they are enemies of the cross of Christ. Their end is ruin, their god is their belly, their glory is in their shame, they mind the things of earth. But our citizenship is in heaven from which also we eagerly await a Savior, our Lord Jesus Christ, who will refashion the body of our lowliness, conforming it to the body of his glory by exerting the power by which he is able also to subject all things to himself.

So then, my brethren, beloved and longed for, my joy and my crown, stand fast thus in the Lord, beloved.

CONCLUSION

In entreat Evodia and I exhort Syntyche to be of one mind in the Lord. And I beseech thee also, my loyal comrade, help them, for they have toiled with me in the gospel, as have Clement and the rest of my fellow-workers whose names are in the book of life.

Rejoice in the Lord always; again I say, rejoice. Let your moderation be known to all men. The Lord is near. Have no anxiety, but in every prayer and supplication with thanksgiving let your petitions be made known to God. And may the peace of God which surpasses all understanding guard your hearts and your minds in Christ Jesus.

For the rest, brethren, whatever things are true, whatever honorable, whatever just, whatever holy, whatever lovable, whatever of good repute, if there be any virtue, if anything worthy of praise, think upon these things. And what you have learned and received and heard and seen in me, these things practise. And the God of peace will be with you.

I rejoiced in the Lord greatly that now at last your concern for me has revived. Indeed you were always concerned, but lacked opportunity.

Not that I speak because I was in want. For I have learned to be self-sufficing in whatever circumstances I am. I know how to live humbly and I know how to live in abundance (I have been schooled to every place and every condition), to be filled and to be hungry, to have abundance and to suffer want. I can do all things in him who strengthens me. Still, you have done well by sharing in my affliction. But, Philippians, you yourselves also know that in the first days of the gospel, when I left Macedonia, no church went into partnership with me in the matter of giving and receiving but you only.

For even in Thessalonica, you sent once and twice something for my need. Not that I am eager for the gift, but I am eager for the profit accumulating to your account. I have all and more than enough. I am fully supplied now that I have received from Epaphroditus what you have sent, a sweet odor, an acceptable sacrifice, well pleasing to God. But may my God supply your every need according to his riches in glory in Christ Jesus. Now to our God and Father be glory for endless ages. Amen.

Greet every saint in Christ Jesus. The brethren with me here greet you. All the saints greet you, especially those of Caesar's household. The grace of our Lord Jesus Christ be with your spirit. Amen.

A Note about
The Epistle of St. Paul the Apostle
to the Colossians

During Paul's stay at Ephesus from about A.D. 53 to 56, the message of the Gospel was carried inland by his zealous converts. Among these was Epaphras, who evangelized the towns of Colossae, Laodicea and Hierapolis, situated in the valley of the Lycus River little more than a hundred miles east of Ephesus. The Apostle took a personal interest in the work of his disciple. A few years later, while he was being detained at Rome for trial before Caesar, he had news of the Colossians through Epaphras. Though the report was, on the whole, favorable, he saw dangerous tendencies in the young Christian community. Self-appointed teachers claimed for angels a very high place of honor and boasted of a deeper knowledge of Christianity, insisting on Judaic observances and a false asceticism. Concerned lest his work be destroyed, Epaphras had come to Rome to seek help from Paul.

Paul met the danger by sending (A.D. 63) a letter to Colossae, borne by Tychicus. To counter the errors, he set forth in clear terms the true doctrine concerning Christ, our Redeemer, head of the mystical body, the Church, and drew up rules for an ideal Christian life. Between these positive sections, the Apostle inserted a vigorous condemnation of the false teachings. Because of the emphatic statement of Christ's divinity that they contain, the first two chapters of the letter are of great doctrinal importance.

The Epistle to the Colossians bears a remarkable resemblance to the Epistle to the Ephesians. Most of the words and phrases of this shorter letter are met with in the other also. Written at the same time, both were addressed to communities of Jewish and pagan converts, struggling in like circumstances to maintain the purity of their faith. The two Epistles should be read and studied together.

The Epistle of St. Paul the Apostle
to the Colossians

INTRODUCTION

Paul, an apostle of Jesus Christ by the will of God, and our brother Timothy, to the brethren in Colossae, holy and faithful in Christ Jesus: grace be to you and peace from God our Father.

We give thanks to the God and Father of our Lord Jesus Christ, praying always for you, for we have heard of your faith in Christ Jesus and of the love that you bear towards all the saints because of the hope that is laid up for you in heaven. Of that hope you have heard in the word of the gospel truth which has reached you, even as it is in the whole world, both bearing fruit and growing; just as it does among you since the day that you heard and recognized the grace of God in truth. Thus you learned from our most dear fellow-servant Epaphras. He is a faithful minister of Christ Jesus in your behalf; and it was he who made known to us your love in the Spirit.

This is why we too have been praying for you unceasingly, since the day we heard this, and asking that you may be filled with knowledge of his will, in all spiritual wisdom and understanding. May you walk worthily of God and please him in all things, bearing fruit in every good work and growing in the knowledge of God. May you be completely strengthened through his glorious power unto perfect patience and long-suffering; joyfully rendering thanks to the Father, who has made us worthy to share the lot of the saints in light. He has rescued us from the power of darkness and transferred us into the kingdom of his beloved Son, in whom we have our redemption, the remission of our sins.

I. THE PRE-EMINENCE OF CHRIST

He is the image of the invisible God, the firstborn of every creature. For in him were created all things in the heavens and on the earth, things visible and things invisible, whether Thrones, or Dominations, or Principalities, or Powers. All things have been created through and unto him, and he is before all creatures, and in him all things hold together. Again, he is the head of his body, the Church; he, who is the beginning, the firstborn from the dead, that in all things he may have the first place. For it has pleased God the Father that in him all his fullness should dwell, and that through him he should reconcile to himself all things, whether on the earth or in the heavens, making peace through the blood of his cross.

You yourselves were at one time estranged and enemies in mind through your evil works. But now he has reconciled you in his body of flesh through his death, to present you holy and undefiled and irreproachable before him. Only you must remain firmly founded in the faith and steadfast and not withdrawing from the hope of the gospel which you have heard. It has been preached to every creature under heaven; and of it I, Paul, have become a minister.

I rejoice now in the sufferings I bear for your sake; and what is lacking of the sufferings of Christ I fill up in my flesh for his body, which is the Church; whose minister I have become in virtue of the office that God has given me in your regard. For I am to preach the word of God fully—the mystery which has been hidden for ages and generations, but now is clearly shown to his saints. To them God willed to make known how rich in glory is this mystery among the Gentiles—Christ in you, your hope of glory! Him we preach, admonishing every man and teaching every man in all wisdom, that we may present every man perfect in Christ Jesus. At this, too, I work and strive, according to the power which he mightily exerts in me.

For I wish you to know what great concern I have for you and for the Laodiceans and for all who have not seen me in the flesh; that their hearts may be comforted, and they themselves well equipped in charity and in all the riches of complete understanding, so as to know the mystery of God the Father of Christ Jesus, in whom are hidden all the treasures of wisdom and knowledge.

II. WARNINGS AGAINST FALSE TEACHERS

Now I say this so that no one may deceive you by persuasive words. For though I am absent in body, yet in spirit I am with you, rejoicing at the sight of your orderly array and the steadfastness of your faith in Christ. Therefore, as you have received Jesus Christ our Lord, so walk in him; be rooted in him and built up on him, and strengthened in the faith, as you also have learnt, rendering thanks abundantly.

See to it that no one deceives you by philosophy and vain deceit, according to human traditions, according to the elements of the world and not according to Christ. For in him dwells all the fullness of the Godhead bodily, and in him who is the head of every Principality and Power you have received of that fullness. In him, too, you have been circumcised with a circumcision not wrought by hand, but through putting off the body of the flesh, a circumcision which is of Christ. For you were buried together with him in Baptism, and in him also rose again through faith in the working of God who raised him from the dead. And you, when you were dead by reason of your sins and the uncircumcision of your flesh, he brought to life along with him, forgiving you all your sins, cancelling the decree against us, which was hostile to us. Indeed, he has taken it completely away, nailing it to the cross. Disarming the Principalities and Powers, he displayed them openly, leading them away in triumph by force of it.

Let no one, then, call you to account for what you eat or drink or in regard to a festival or a new moon or a Sabbath. These are a shadow of things to come, but the substance is of Christ. Let no one cheat you who takes pleasure in self-abasement and worship of the angels, and enters vainly into what he has not seen, puffed up by his mere human mind. Such a one is not united to the head, from whom the whole body, supplied and built up by joints and ligaments, attains a growth that is of God.

If you have died with Christ to the elements of the world, why, as if still living in the world, do you lay down the rules: "Do not touch; nor taste; nor handle!"—things that must all perish in their very use? In this you follow "the precepts and doctrines of men," which, to be sure, have a show of wisdom in superstition and self-abasement and hard treatment of the body, but are not to be held in esteem, and lead to the full gratification of the flesh.

Therefore, if you have risen with Christ, seek the things that are above, where Christ is seated at the right hand of God. Mind the things that are above, not the things that are on earth. For you have died and your life is hidden with Christ in God. When Christ, your life, shall appear, then you too will appear with him in glory.

III. THE IDEAL CHRISTIAN LIFE IN THE WORLD

Therefore mortify your members, which are on earth: immorality, uncleanness, lust, evil desire and covetousness (which is a form of idol-worship). Because of these things the wrath of God comes upon the unbelievers, and you yourselves once walked in them when they were your life. But now do you also put them all away: anger, wrath, malice, abusive language and foul-mouthed utterances. Do not lie to one another. Strip off the old man with his deeds and put on the new, one that is being renewed unto perfect knowledge "according to the image of his Creator." Here there is not "Gentile and Jew," "circumcised and uncircumcised," "Barbarian and Scythian," "slave and freeman"; but Christ is all things and in all.

Put on therefore, as God's chosen ones, holy and beloved, a heart of mercy, kindness, humility, meekness, patience. Bear with one another and forgive one another, if anyone has a grievance against any other; even as the Lord has forgiven you, so also do you forgive. But above all these things have charity, which is the bond of perfection. And may the peace of Christ reign in your hearts; unto that peace, indeed, you were called in one body. Show yourselves thankful. Let the word of Christ dwell in you abundantly: in all wisdom teach and admonish one another by psalms, hymns and spiritual songs, singing in your hearts to God by his grace. Whatever you do in word or in work, do all in the name of the Lord Jesus, giving thanks to God the Father through him.

Wives, be subject to your husbands, as is becoming in the Lord. Husbands, love your wives and do not be bitter towards them. Children, obey your parents in all things, for that is pleasing in the Lord. Fathers, do not provoke your children to anger, that they may not be discouraged.

Slaves, obey in all things your masters according to the flesh; not with eye-service seeking to please men, but in singleness of heart from fear of the Lord. Whatever you do, work at it from the heart as for the Lord and not for men, knowing that from the Lord you will receive the inheritance as your reward. Serve the Lord Christ. For he who does a wrong will reap the wrong he did, and there is no respect of persons.

Masters, give your slaves what is just and fair, know that you too have a Master in heaven.

Be assiduous in prayer, being wakeful therein with thanksgiving. At the same time pray for us also, that God may give us an opportunity for the word, to announce the mystery of Christ (for which also I am in chains), that I may openly announce it as I ought to speak. Walk in wisdom as regards outsiders, making the most of your time. Let your speech, while always attractive, be seasoned with salt, that you may know how you ought to answer each other.

CONCLUSION

All my circumstances Tychicus, our dearest brother and faithful minister and fellow-servant in the Lord, will tell you. Him I have sent to you for this very purpose, that he may learn your circumstances and comfort your hearts. With him is Onesimus, our most dear and faithful brother, who is one of you. They will tell you all that is going on here.

Aristarchus, my fellow-prisoner, sends you greetings; so does Mark, Barnabas' cousin (concerning whom you have received instructions—if he comes to you, welcome him), and Jesus who is called Justus. Of men circumcised, these only are my fellow-workers in the kingdom of God; they have been a comfort to me. Epaphras, who is one of you, sends you greetings—a servant of Christ Jesus, who is ever solicitous for you in his prayers, that you may remain perfect and completely in accord with all the will of God. Yes, I bear him witness that he labors much for you and for those who are at Laodicea and at Hierapolis. Luke, our most dear physician, and Demas send you greetings.

Greetings to the brethren who are at Laodicea and to Nymphas and the church that is in his house. And when this letter has been read among you, see that it be read in the church of the Laodiceans also; and that you yourselves read the letter from Laodicea. And say to Archippus: "Look to the ministry which thou hast received in the Lord, that thou fulfill it."

I, Paul, greet you by my own hand. Remember my chains. Grace be with you. Amen.

A Note *about*
The First Epistle of St. Paul the Apostle
to the Thessalonians

St. Paul founded the church at Thessalonica during the early part of his second great missionary journey, i.e., about A.D. 51. Thessalonica, the capital of Macedonia, was a large and important city. Its population was predominantly Gentile, but Jews dwelt there in sufficient numbers to have a synagogue. Paul succeeded in converting some of the Jews and a large number of Gentiles. But his success stirred up the envy of the unbelieving Jews, who by calumny and riot compelled him to flee to Beroea. From there he went to Athens and Corinth, and it was in the latter city that this letter was written.

While at Athens, Paul, fearing lest the persecution which continued against the church at Thessalonica should cause his new converts to abandon the faith, sent Timothy to ascertain conditions in the church and to comfort and strengthen its members. Timothy reported to Paul at Corinth, bringing the cheering news of their constancy in the face of persecution. He likewise informed Paul that the Thessalonians required further instruction on the Second Coming of Christ, and this topic forms the main doctrinal subject of the Epistle, which was written shortly after Timothy's return from Thessalonica. The Second Epistle to the Thessalonians was written soon after the First, and these two Epistles are generally regarded as the earliest of Paul's writings.

The First Epistle of St. Paul the Apostle
to the Thessalonians

INTRODUCTION

Paul and Silvanus and Timothy, to the church of the Thessalonians in God the Father and in the Lord Jesus Christ: grace be to you and peace.

We give thanks to God always for you all, continually making a remembrance of you in our prayers; being mindful before God our Father of your work of faith, and labor, and charity, and your enduring hope in our Lord Jesus Christ.

We know, brethren, beloved of God, how you were chosen. For our gospel was not delivered to you in word only, but in power also, and in the Holy Spirit, and in much fullness, as indeed you know what manner of men we have been among you for your sakes. And you became imitators of us and of the Lord, receiving the word in great tribulation, with joy of the Holy Spirit, so that you became a pattern to all the believers in Macedonia and in Achaia. For from you the word of the Lord has been spread abroad, not only in Macedonia and Achaia, but in every place your faith in God has gone forth, so that we need say nothing further.

For they themselves report concerning us how we entered among you, and how you turned to God from idols, to serve the living and true God, and to await from heaven Jesus, his Son, whom he raised from the dead, who has delivered us from the wrath to come.

I. PAUL'S PAST RELATIONS
AND PRESENT INTEREST

For you yourselves, brethren, know that our coming among you was not in vain. But although we had previously experienced suffering and shameful treatment at Philippi, as you know, we had confidence in our God to preach to you the gospel of God amid much anxiety. For our exhortation was not from error, nor from impure motives, nor from guile. But as approved by God to be entrusted with the gospel, so we speak not as pleasing men, but God, who proves our hearts. For at no time have we used words of flattery, as you know, nor any pretext for avarice, God is witness, nor have we sought glory from men, neither from you nor from others. Although as the apostles of Christ, we could have claimed a position of honor among you, still while in your midst we were as children: as if a nurse were cherishing her own children, so we in our love for you would gladly have imparted to you not only the gospel of God, but also our own souls; because you had become most dear to us.

For you remember, brethren, our labor and toil. We worked night and day so as not to be a burden to any of you while we preached to you the gospel of God. You are witnesses and God also, how holy and just and blameless was our conduct towards you who have believed; inasmuch as you are aware of how we entreated and comforted each one of you, acting towards you as a father towards his children, declaring to you that you should walk worthily of God, who called you unto his kingdom and glory.

Therefore we too give thanks to God without ceasing, because when you heard and received from us the word of God, you welcomed it not as the word of men, but, as it truly is, the word of God, who works in you who have believed. For you, brethren, have become imitators of the churches of God which are in Judea in Christ Jesus, in that you also have suffered the same things from your own countrymen as they have from the Jews, who both killed the Lord Jesus and the prophets, and have persecuted us. They are displeasing to God, and are hostile to all men, because they hinder us from speaking to the Gentiles, that they may be saved. Thus they are always filling up the measure of their sins, for the wrath of God has come upon them to the utmost.

But we, brethren, being bereaved of you for a short time, in sight, not in heart, have made more than ordinary efforts to hasten to see you, so great has been our desire. For we wanted to come to you—I, Paul, more than once—but Satan hindered us. For what is our hope, or joy, or crown of glory, if not you before our Lord Jesus Christ at his coming? Yes, you are our glory and joy.

And so when we could bear it no longer we decided to remain at Athens alone, and we sent Timothy, our brother and a servant of God in the gospel of Christ, to strengthen and comfort you in your faith, lest any should be shaken by these tribulations. For you yourselves know that we are appointed thereto. Indeed even when we were with you we used to tell you that we should suffer tribulations, as also it has come to pass, and you know. Consequently when I could bear it no longer I sent in order to know your faith, lest perhaps the tempter might have tempted you, and our labor might come to naught.

But now that Timothy has come to us from you, and has made known to us your faith and charity, and your kindly remembrance of us at all times, and that you long to see us just as we long to see you, we have accordingly found comfort in you, brethren, amid all our trials and tribulations, on account of your faith; because now we live, if you stand fast in the Lord. For what thanks can we return to God for you for all the joy wherewith we rejoice for your sakes before our God? Night and day we pray more and more that we may see you again, and may supply those things that are lacking to your faith.

May God our Father and our Lord Jesus direct our way unto you. And may the Lord make you to increase and abound in charity towards one another, and towards all men just as we do towards you, that he may strengthen your hearts, blameless in holiness before God our Father, at the coming of our Lord Jesus Christ, with all his saints. Amen.

Moreover, brethren, even as you have learned from us how you ought to walk to please God—as indeed you are walking—we beseech and exhort you in the Lord Jesus to make even greater progress. For you know what precepts I have given to you by the Lord Jesus. For this is the will of God, your sanctification; that you abstain from immorality, that every one of you learn how to possess his vessel in holiness and honor, not in the passion of lust like the Gentiles who do not know God; that no one transgress and overreach his brother in the matter, because the Lord is the avenger of all these things, as we have told you before and have testified. For God has not called us unto uncleanness, but unto holiness. Therefore, he who rejects these things rejects not man but God, who has also given his Holy Spirit to us.

But concerning brotherly charity there is no need for us to write to you, for you yourselves have learned from God to love one another. For indeed you practise it towards all the brethren all over Macedonia. But we exhort you, brethren, to make even greater progress. Strive to live peacefully, minding your own affairs, working with your own hands, as we charged you, so that you may walk becomingly towards outsiders, and may need nothing.

II. THE SECOND COMING OF OUR LORD

But we would not, brethren, have you ignorant concerning those who are asleep, lest you should grieve, even as others who have no hope. For if we believe that Jesus died and rose again, so with him God will bring those also who have fallen asleep through Jesus. For this we say to you in the word of the Lord, that we who live, who survive until the coming of the Lord, shall not precede those who have fallen asleep. For the Lord himself with cry of command, with voice of archangel, and with trumpet of God will descend from heaven; and the dead in Christ will rise up first. Then we who live, who survive, shall be caught up together with them in clouds to meet the Lord in the air, and so we shall ever be with the Lord. Wherefore, comfort one another with these words.

But of the times and seasons, brethren, you have no need that we write to you, for you yourselves know well that the day of the Lord is to come as a thief in the night. For when they shall say, "Peace and security," even then sudden destruction will come upon them, as birth pangs upon her who is with child, and they will not escape.

But you, brethren, are not in darkness, that that day should overtake you as a thief; for you are all children of the light and children of the day. We are not of night, nor of darkness. Therefore, let us not sleep as do the rest, but let us be wakeful and sober. For they who sleep, sleep at night, and they who are drunk, are drunk at night. But let us, who are of the day, be sober. Let us put on the breastplate of faith and charity, and for a helmet the hope of salvation. For God has not destined us unto wrath, but to gain salvation through our Lord Jesus Christ, who died for us in order that, whether we wake or sleep, we should live together with him. Wherefore, comfort one another and edify one another, even as indeed you do.

CONCLUSION

Now we beseech you, brethren, to appreciate those who labor among you, and who are over you in the Lord and admonish you. Esteem them with a more abundant love on account of their work. Be at peace with them. And we exhort you, brethren, reprove the irregular, comfort the faint-hearted, support the weak, be patient towards all men. See that no one renders evil for evil to any man; but always strive after good towards one another and towards all men.

Rejoice always. Pray without ceasing. In all things give thanks; for this is the will of God in Christ Jesus regarding you all. Do not extinguish the Spirit. Do not despise prophecies. But test all things; hold fast that which is good. Keep yourselves from every kind of evil.

And may the God of peace himself sanctify you completely, and may your spirit and soul and body be preserved sound, blameless at the coming of our Lord Jesus Christ. He who called you is faithful and will do this.

Brethren, pray for us. Greet all the brethren with a holy kiss. I charge you by the Lord that this epistle be read to all the holy brethren. The grace of our Lord Jesus Christ be with you. Amen.

A Note *about*
The Second Epistle of St. Paul the Apostle
to the Thessalonians

The First Epistle failed to quiet the doubts and fears of the Thessalonians, and so Paul hastened to supply them with fuller information on the subject of the *parousia*, or Second Coming of Christ. He informed them that the *parousia* was not at hand. It could not take place until a great apostasy occurred and Antichrist appeared. Some of the Thessalonians who were convinced that the Second Coming of Christ was at hand thought it useless to work and consequently lived irregularly. Paul condemned this practice and ordered the offenders to be corrected. He urged all to adhere to his teachings, whether these were given orally or in writing.

The Second Epistle of St. Paul the Apostle
to the Thessalonians

INTRODUCTION

Paul and Silvanus and Timothy, to the church of the Thessalonians in God our Father and the Lord Jesus Christ: grace be to you and peace from God our Father and the Lord Jesus Christ.

We are bound to give thanks to God always for you, brethren. It is fitting that we should, because your faith grows exceedingly and your charity each one for the other increases. And because of this we ourselves boast of you in the churches of God for your patience and faith in all your persecutions and the tribulations that you are enduring. In this there is a proof of the just judgment of God counting you worthy of the kingdom of God, for which also you suffer. Indeed it is just on the part of God to repay with affliction those who afflict you, and to give you who are afflicted rest with us at the revelation of the Lord Jesus, who will come from heaven with the angels of his power, in flaming fire, to inflict punishment on those who do not know God, and who do not obey the gospel of our Lord Jesus Christ.

These will be punished with eternal ruin, away from the face of the Lord and the glory of his power, when on that day he shall come to be glorified in his saints, and to be marveled at in all those who have believed. For our testimony before you has been believed.

To this end also we pray always for you, that our God may make you worthy of his calling, and may fulfill with power every good purpose and work of faith, that the name of our Lord Jesus Christ may be glorified in you, and you in him, according to the grace of our God and the Lord Jesus Christ.

I. THE SECOND COMING OF OUR LORD

We beseech you, brethren, by the coming of our Lord Jesus Christ and our being gathered together unto him, not to be hastily shaken from your right mind, nor terrified, whether by spirit, or by utterance, or by letter attributed to us, as though the day of the Lord were near at hand. Let no one deceive you in any way, for the day of the Lord will not come unless the apostasy comes first, and the man of sin is revealed, the son of perdition, who opposes and is exalted above all that is called God, or that is worshipped, so that he sits in the temple of God and gives himself out as if he were God. Do you not remember that when I was still with you, I used to tell you these things? And now you know what restrains him, that he may be revealed in his proper time. For the mystery of iniquity is already at work; provided only that he who is at present restraining it, does still restrain, until he is gotten out of the way.

And then the wicked one will be revealed, whom the Lord Jesus will slay with the breath of his mouth and will destroy with the brightness of his coming.

And his coming is according to the working of Satan with all power and signs and lying wonders, and with all wicked deception to those who are perishing. For they have not received the love of truth that they might be saved. Therefore God sends them a misleading influence that they may believe falsehood, that all may be judged who have not believed the truth, but have preferred wickedness.

But we, brethren beloved of God, are bound to give thanks to God always for you, because God has chosen you as first-fruits unto salvation through the sanctification of the Spirit and belief of the truth. For this purpose he also called you by our preaching to gain the glory of our Lord Jesus Christ. So then, brethren, stand firm, and hold the teachings that you have learned, whether by word or by letter of ours. And may our Lord Jesus Christ himself and God our Father, who has loved us and has given us through grace everlasting consolation and good hope, comfort and strengthen your hearts in every good work and word.

II. EXHORTATION

In conclusion, brethren, pray for us, that the word of the Lord may run and be glorified even as among you, and that we may be delivered from troublesome and evil men; for not all men have the faith.

But the Lord is faithful, who will strengthen you and guard you from evil. And we have confidence in the Lord as regards you, that you both do and will do the things that we enjoin. And may the Lord direct your hearts into the love of God and the patience of Christ.

And we charge you, brethren, in the name of our Lord Jesus Christ, to withdraw yourselves from every brother who lives irregularly, and not according to the teaching received from us. For you yourselves know how you ought to imitate us; for we were not unruly while with you, neither did we eat any man's bread at his cost, but we worked night and day in labor and toil, so that we might not burden any of you. Not that we did not have the right to do so, but that we might make ourselves an example for you to imitate us. For indeed when we were with you we used to charge you: If any man will not work, neither let him eat. For we have heard that some among you are living irregularly, doing no work but busy at meddling. Now such persons we charge and exhort in the Lord Jesus Christ that they work quietly and eat their own bread.

But you, brethren, do not grow tired of well-doing. And if anyone does not obey our word by this letter, note that man and do not associate with him, that he may be put to shame. Yet do not regard him as an enemy, but admonish him as a brother.

CONCLUSION

And may the Lord of peace himself give you everlasting peace in every place. The Lord be with you all. I, Paul, greet you with my own hand. This is the mark in every letter. Thus I write. The grace of our Lord Jesus Christ be with you all. Amen.

A Note *about*
The First Epistle of St. Paul the Apostle
to Timothy

The two Epistles to St. Timothy and the one to St. Titus are called Pastoral Epistles because they are addressed directly, not to any church as a group, but rather to its head or pastor for his guidance in the rule of the church. All three Epistles are closely connected in form and content.

St. Timothy was of Lystra in Lycaonia, born of a Greek father and a Jewish mother. His mother Eunice and his grandmother Lois, as well as Timothy himself, probably embraced the faith during St. Paul's first stay at Lystra, since they were already Christians at his return on the second missionary journey. It was at that time that Timothy was highly recommended by the Christians, and the Apostle chose him as a missionary companion. Thereafter Timothy was seldom parted from St. Paul, who employed him in some difficult and confidential missions. During the first imprisonment of the Apostle at Rome, Timothy was with his master. After this imprisonment he accompanied the Apostle on his last missionary journey and was left at Ephesus to take charge of the church there. The Apostle shortly before his death wrote Timothy to come to him before the winter.

This first Epistle was written between Paul's liberation from the first imprisonment (A.D. 63) and his death (A.D. 67).

A twofold thought is dominant in this Epistle. Timothy must energetically combat false teachers and actively engage in the work of organizing the community. The thought of the Apostle moves restlessly back and forth on these two points, since he was fully aware from his own experience of the dangers that threatened.

The First Epistle of St. Paul the Apostle to Timothy

INTRODUCTION

Paul, an apostle of Jesus Christ, by the order of God our Savior, and of Christ Jesus our hope, to Timothy, his beloved son in the faith: grace, mercy and peace from God the Father and from Christ Jesus our Lord.

I. AGAINST FALSE TEACHERS

When I went to Macedonia, I asked thee to stay on at Ephesus that thou mightest charge some not to teach novel doctrines, and not to study fables and endless genealogies which beget controversies rather than godly edification, which is in the faith. Now the purpose of this charge is charity, from a pure heart and a good conscience and faith unfeigned. Some going astray from these things have turned aside to vain babbling, desiring to be teachers of the Law, when they understand neither what they say nor the things about which they make assertion.

But we know that the Law is good, if a man uses it rightly, knowing that the Law is not made for the just, but for the unjust and rebellious, for the ungodly and sinners, for criminals and the defiled, for parricides and matricides, for murderers, for immoral people, for sodomites, for kidnappers, for liars, for perjurers, and whatever else is contrary to the sound doctrine, according to the gospel of the glory of the blessed God, which has been committed to my trust.

I give thanks to Christ Jesus our Lord, who has strengthened me, because he counted me trustworthy in making me his minister. For I formerly was a blasphemer, a persecutor and a bitter adversary; but I obtained the mercy of God because I acted ignorantly, in unbelief. Indeed, the grace of our Lord has abounded beyond measure in the faith and love that is in Christ Jesus. This saying is true and worthy of entire acceptance, that Jesus Christ came into the world to save sinners, of whom I am the chief. But for this reason I obtained mercy, that in me first Christ Jesus might show forth all patience, as an example to those who shall believe in him for the attainment of life everlasting. To the King of the ages, who is immortal, invisible, the one only God, be honor and glory forever and ever. Amen.

I commit to thee this charge, my son Timothy, that according to the prophecies once made concerning thee, thou mayest fight the good fight by means of them, having faith and a good conscience. Some rejecting this have made shipwreck of the faith, among whom are Hymeneus and Alexander, whom I have delivered up to Satan that they may learn not to blaspheme.

II. PASTORAL CHARGE

I urge therefore, first of all, that supplications, prayers, intercessions and thanksgivings be made for all men; for kings, and for all in high positions, that we may lead a quiet and peaceful life in all piety and worthy behavior. This is good and agreeable in the sight of God our Savior, who wishes all men to be saved and to come to the knowledge of the truth. For there is one God, and one Mediator between God and men, himself man, Christ Jesus, who gave himself a ransom for all, bearing witness in his own time. To this I have been appointed a preacher and an apostle (I tell the truth, I do not lie), a teacher of the Gentiles in faith and truth.

I wish, then, that the men pray everywhere, lifting up pure hands, without wrath and contention. In like manner I wish women to be decently dressed, adorning themselves with modesty and dignity, not with braided hair or gold or pearls or expensive clothing, but with good works such as become women professing godliness. Let a woman learn in silence with all submission. For I do not allow a woman to teach, or to exercise authority over men; but she is to keep quiet. For Adam was formed first, then Eve. And Adam was not deceived, but the woman was deceived and was in sin. Yet women will be saved by childbearing, if they continue in faith and love and holiness with modesty.

This saying is true: If anyone is eager for the office of bishop, he desires a good work. A bishop then, must be blameless, married but once, reserved, prudent, of good conduct, hospitable, a teacher, not a drinker or a brawler, but moderate, not quarrelsome, not avaricious. He should rule well his own household, keeping his children under control and perfectly respectful. For if a man cannot rule his own household, how is he to take care of the church of God? He must not be a new convert, lest he be puffed up with pride and incur the condemnation passed on the devil. Besides this he must have a good reputation with those who are outside, that he may not fall into disgrace and into a snare of the devil.

Deacons also must be honorable, not double-tongued, not given to much wine, not greedy for base gain, but holding the mystery of faith in a pure conscience. And let them first be tried, and if found without reproach let them be allowed to serve. In like manner let the women be honorable, not slanderers, but reserved, faithful in all things. Deacons should be men who have been married but once, ruling well their children and their own households. And those who have fulfilled well this office will acquire a good position and great confidence in the faith that is in Christ Jesus.

III. AGAINST FALSE DOCTRINE

I write these things to thee hoping to come to thee shortly, but in order that thou mayest know, if I am delayed, how to conduct thyself in the house of God, which is the Church of the living God, the pillar and mainstay of the truth. And obviously great is the mystery of godliness: which was manifested in the flesh, was justified in the spirit, appeared to angels, was preached to Gentiles, believed in the world, taken up in glory.

Now the Spirit expressly says that in after times some will depart from the faith, giving heed to deceitful spirits and doctrines of devils, speaking lies hypocritically, and having their conscience branded. They will forbid marriage, and will enjoin abstinence from foods, which God has created to be partaken of with thanksgiving by the faithful and by those who know the truth. For every creature of God is good, and nothing is to be rejected that is accepted with thanksgiving. For it is sanctified by the word of God and prayer.

By recommending these things to the brethren, thou wilt be a good minister of Christ Jesus, nourished with the words of faith and of the good doctrine to which thou hast attained. But avoid foolish fables and old wives' tales and train thyself in godliness. For bodily training is of little profit, while godliness is profitable in all respects, since it has the promise of the present life as well as of that which is to come. This saying is true and worthy of entire acceptance; for we work and are reviled for this reason, that we hope in the living God, who is the Savior of all men, especially of believers.

Command and teach these things. Let no man despise thy youth, but be thou an example to the faithful in speech, in conduct, in charity, in faith, in chastity. Until I come, be diligent in reading, in exhortation and in teaching. Do not neglect the grace that is in thee, granted to thee by reason of prophecy with the laying on of hands of the presbyterate. Meditate on these things, give thyself entirely to them, that thy progress may be manifest to all. Take heed to thyself and to thy teaching, be earnest in them. For in so doing thou wilt save both thyself and those who hear thee.

IV. DUTIES TOWARDS THE FLOCK

Do not rebuke an elderly man, but exhort him as you would a father, and young men as brothers, elderly women as mothers, younger women as sisters in all chastity.

Honor widows who are truly widowed. But if a widow has children or grandchildren, let these first learn to provide for their own household and make some return to their parents, for this is pleasing to God. But she who is truly a widow, and left solitary, has set her hope on God and continues in supplications and prayers night and day. For she who gives herself up to pleasures is dead while she is still alive. And command them to be blameless. But if anyone does not take care of his own, and especially of his household, he has denied the faith and is worse than an unbeliever.

Let a widow who is selected be not less than sixty years old, having been married but once, with a reputation for her good works in bringing up children, in practising hospitality, in washing the saints' feet, in helping those in trouble, in carefully pursuing every good work. But refuse younger widows, for when they have wantonly turned away from Christ, they wish to marry, and are to be condemned because they have broken their first troth. And further, being idle, they learn to go about from house to house, and are not only idle but gossipers as well and busybodies, mentioning things they ought not. I desire therefore that the younger widows marry, bear children, rule their households, and give the adversary no occasion for abusing us. For already some have turned aside after Satan. If any believing woman has widowed relatives, let her provide for them and do not let the Church be burdened, in order that there may be enough for those who are truly widows.

Let the presbyters who rule well be held worthy of double honor, especially those who labor in the word and in teaching. For Scripture says, "Thou shalt not muzzle the ox that treads out the grain," and, "The laborer is worthy of his wages." Do not listen to an accusation against a presbyter unless it is supported by two or three witnesses. When they sin, rebuke them in the presence of all, that the rest also may have fear. I charge thee before God and Christ Jesus and the elect angels that thou observe these things impartially, in no way favoring either side. Do not lay hands hastily upon anyone, and do not be a partner in other men's sins. Keep thyself chaste. Stop drinking water only, but use a little wine for thy stomach's sake and thy frequent infirmities. Some men's sins are manifest even before investigation, other men's sins only afterwards. In like manner also the good works are manifest, and those that are otherwise cannot be hidden.

Let slaves who are under the yoke account their masters deserving of all honor, that the name of the Lord and his teaching be not blasphemed. And when they have masters who are believers, let them not despise them because they are brethren, but let them serve them all the more because they who receive their service are believers and beloved. Teach and exhort these things.

If anyone teaches otherwise and does not agree with the sound instruction of our Lord Jesus Christ, and that doctrine which is according to godliness, he is proud, knowing nothing, but doting about controversies and disputes of words. From these arise envies, quarrels, blasphemies, base suspicions, the wranglings of men corrupt in mind and bereft of truth, supposing godliness to be gain. And godliness with contentment is indeed great gain. For we brought nothing into the world, and certainly we can take nothing out; but having food and sufficient clothing, with these let us be content. But those who seek to become rich fall into temptation and a snare and into many useless and harmful desires, which plunge men into destruction and damnation. For covetousness is the root of all evils, and some in their eagerness to get rich have strayed from the faith and have involved themselves in many troubles.

But thou, O man of God, flee these things; but pursue justice, godliness, faith, charity, patience, mildness. Fight the good fight of the faith, lay hold on the life eternal, to which thou hast been called, and hast made the good confession before many witnesses. I charge thee in the sight of God, who gives life to all things, and in the sight of Christ Jesus, who bore witness before Pontius Pilate to the good confession, that thou keep the commandment without stain, blameless until the coming of our Lord Jesus Christ. This coming he in his own time will make manifest, who is the Blessed and only Sovereign, the King of kings and Lord of lords; who alone has immortality and dwells in light inaccessible, whom no man has seen or can see, to whom be honor and everlasting dominion. Amen.

Charge the rich of this world not to be proud, or to trust in the uncertainty of riches, but in God, who provides all things in abundance for their enjoyment. Let them do good and be rich in good works, giving readily, sharing with others, and thus providing for themselves a good foundation against the time to come, in order that they may lay hold on the true life.

CONCLUSION

O Timothy, guard the trust and keep free from profane novelties in speech and the contradictions of so-called knowledge, which some have professed and have fallen away from the faith. Grace be with thee. Amen.

A Note *about*
The Second Epistle of St. Paul the Apostle
to Timothy

The Second Epistle to Timothy was written in A.D. 66 or
67, while St. Paul was a prisoner in Rome for the second
and last time.

The Apostle describes himself as still in prison and abandoned by nearly all his companions, who for various rea-
sons have left Rome. Only Luke the physician, of whom he
seems to have special need, is with him (4:11). He feels his
isolation keenly, particularly since his relations with the Roman church are much restricted. He feels the need of seeing
Mark and Timothy, for whom Tychicus was to substitute
at Ephesus (4:11f). He sees his death near (4:6–8). The Epistle is an urgent invitation to Timothy to join him, yet the
Apostle is concerned to strengthen the spirit of his beloved
disciple and to urge him again to act energetically against
the separatist teachers.

The Second Epistle of St. Paul the Apostle to Timothy

INTRODUCTION

Paul, an apostle of Jesus Christ, by the will of God, in accordance with the promise of life in Christ Jesus, to Timothy, my beloved son: grace, mercy and peace from God the Father and from Christ Jesus our Lord.

I give thanks to God, whom I serve as did my forefathers, with a clear conscience, that I remember thee without ceasing in my prayers night and day. Recalling thy tears, I long to see thee, that I may be filled with joy. I remember that unfeigned faith of thine, which dwelt first in thy grandmother Lois and in thy mother Eunice, and dwells, I am certain, in thee also.

I. PASTORAL CHARGE

For this reason I admonish thee to stir up the grace of God which is in thee by the laying on of my hands. For God has not given us the spirit of fear, but of power and of love and of prudence. Do not, therefore, be ashamed of testimony for our Lord, nor of me, his prisoner, but enter into my sufferings for the gospel through the power of God. He has redeemed us and called us with a holy calling, not according to our works, but according to his own purpose and the grace which was granted to us in Christ Jesus before this world existed, but is now made known by the manifestation of our Savior Jesus Christ. He has destroyed death and brought to light life and incorruption by the gospel, of which I have been appointed a preacher and an apostle and a teacher of the Gentiles. That is why also I am suffering these things; yet I am not ashamed. For I know whom I have believed, and I am certain that he is able to guard the trust committed to me against that day. Hold to the form of sound teaching which thou hast heard from me, in the faith and love which are Christ Jesus. Guard the good trust through the Holy Spirit, who dwells in us.

This thou knowest that all in the province of Asia have turned away from me, among them, Phigelus and Hermogenes. May the Lord grant mercy to the house of Onesiphorus, because he often comforted me and was not ashamed of my chains; but when he came to Rome, he sought me out diligently and found me. May the Lord grant him to find mercy from the Lord on that day. And thou knowest very well the many services he rendered me at Ephesus.

Therefore, my child, be strengthened in the grace which is in Christ Jesus; and the things that thou hast heard from me through many witnesses, commend to trustworthy men who shall be competent in turn to teach others. Conduct thyself in work as a good soldier of Christ Jesus. No one serving as God's soldier entangles himself in worldly affairs, that he may please him whose approval he has secured. And again, one who enters a contest is not crowned unless he has competed according to the rules. The farmer who toils must be the first to partake of the fruits. Take in what I tell thee, for the Lord will give thee understanding in all things.

Remember that Jesus Christ rose from the dead and was descended from David; this is my gospel, in which I suffer even to bonds, as a criminal. But the word of God is not bound. This is why I bear all things for the sake of the elect, that they also may obtain the salvation that is in Christ Jesus, with heavenly glory. This saying is true: If we have died with him, we shall also live with him; if we endure, we shall also reign with him; if we disown him, he also will disown us; if we are faithless, he remains faithful, for he cannot disown himself.

II. FIDELITY TO HIS OFFICE

Recall these things to their mind, charging them in the sight of the Lord not to dispute with words, for that is useless, leading to the ruin of the listeners. Use all care to present thyself to God as a man approved, a worker that cannot be ashamed, rightly handling the word of truth. But avoid profane and empty babblings, for they contribute much to ungodliness, and their speech spreads like a cancer. Of this sort are Hymeneus and Philetus, who have erred from the truth in saying that the resurrection has taken place already; and they are destroying the faith of some.

But the sure foundation of God stands firm, bearing this

seal: "The Lord knows who are his"; and, "Let everyone depart from iniquity who names the name of the Lord."

But in a great house there are vessels not only of gold and silver, but also of wood and clay; and some are for honorable uses, but some for ignoble. If anyone, therefore, has cleansed himself from these, he will be a vessel for honorable uses, sanctified and useful to the Lord, ready for every good work. But flee the cravings of youth and pursue justice, faith, charity and peace with those who call on the Lord from a pure heart. Avoid also foolish and ignorant controversies, knowing that they breed quarrels. But the servant of the Lord must not quarrel, but be gentle towards all, ready to teach, patient, gently admonishing those who resist, in case God should give them repentance to know the truth, and they recover themselves from the snare of the devil, to whose will they are held captive.

But know this, that in the last days dangerous times will come. Men will be lovers of self, covetous, haughty, proud, blasphemers, disobedient to parents, ungrateful, criminal, heartless, faithless, slanderers, incontinent, merciless, unkind, treacherous, stubborn, puffed up with pride, loving pleasure more than God; having a semblance indeed of piety, but disowning its power. Avoid these. For of such are they who make their way into houses and captivate silly women who are sin-laden and led away by various lusts: ever learning yet never attaining knowledge of the truth. Just as Jamnes and Mambres resisted Moses, so these men also resist the truth; for they are corrupt in mind, reprobate as regards the faith. But they will make no further progress, for their folly will be obvious to all, as was that of those others.

But thou hast closely followed my doctrine, my conduct,

my purpose, my faith, my long-suffering, my love, my patience, my persecutions, my afflictions; such as befell me at Antioch, Iconium and Lystra—such persecutions as I suffered, and out of them all the Lord delivered me. And all who want to live piously in Christ Jesus will suffer persecution. But the wicked and impostors will go from bad to worse, erring and leading into error. But do thou continue in the things that thou hast learned and that have been entrusted to thee, knowing of whom thou hast learned them. For from thy infancy thou hast known the Sacred Writings, which are able to instruct thee unto salvation by the faith which is in Christ Jesus. All Scripture is inspired by God and useful for teaching, for reproving, for correcting, for instructing in justice; that the man of God may be perfect, equipped for every good work.

I charge thee, in the sight of God and Christ Jesus, who will judge the living and the dead by his coming and by his kingdom, preach the word, be urgent in season, out of season; reprove, entreat, rebuke with all patience and teaching. For there will come a time when they will not endure the sound doctrine; but having itching ears, will heap up to themselves teachers according to their own lusts, and they will turn away their hearing from the truth and turn aside rather to fables. But do thou be watchful in all things, bear with tribulation patiently, work as a preacher of the gospel, fulfill thy ministry.

As for me, I am already being poured out in sacrifice, and the time of my deliverance is at hand. I have fought the good fight, I have finished the course, I have kept the faith. For the rest, there is laid up for me a crown of justice, which the Lord, the just Judge, will give me in that day; yet not to me only, but also to those who love his coming.

CONCLUSION

Make haste to come to me shortly; for Demas has deserted me, loving this world, and has gone to Thessalonica, Crescens to Galatia, Titus to Dalmatia. Luke only is with me. Take Mark and bring him with thee, for he is useful to me for the ministry. But Tychicus I have sent to Ephesus. When thou comest, bring with thee the cloak that I left at Troas with Carpus, and the books, especially the parchments. Alexander, the coppersmith, has done me much harm; the Lord will render to him according to his deeds. Do thou also avoid him for he has vehemently opposed our words.

At my first defense no one came to my support, but all forsook me; may it not be laid to their charge. But the Lord stood by me and strengthened me, that through me the preaching of the gospel might be completed, and that all the Gentiles might hear; and I was delivered from the lion's mouth. The Lord will deliver me from every work of evil, and will preserve me for his heavenly kingdom; to whom be the glory forever and ever. Amen.

Greet Prisca and Aquila and the household of Onesiphorus. Erastus stayed at Corinth, but Trophimus I left sick at Miletus. Hasten to come before winter. Eubulus, Pudens, Linus and Claudia and all the brethren greet thee. The Lord Jesus Christ be with thy spirit. Grace be with you. Amen.

A Note *about*
The Epistle of St. Paul the Apostle to Titus

St. Titus was born of Greek parents. He accompanied Sts. Paul and Barnabas to the Council of Jerusalem. He was uncircumcised, and although at the Council Judaizers insisted that he submit to this rite, St. Paul refused to permit it. Titus is addressed in this Epistle as "beloved son," probably because he was converted to the faith by the Apostle. He was sent by the latter on several important missions during the third missionary journey. We lose sight of him after this, as he is not mentioned in the Epistles of the Captivity. From this Epistle we learn that St. Paul entrusted him with the organization of the church in Crete. Afterwards he was summoned by the Apostle to Nicopolis in Epirus, and during Paul's final Roman imprisonment he was sent on a mission to Dalmatia. According to tradition, he returned to Crete to exercise his episcopal office and died there.

The journey of St. Paul to the island of Crete cannot be inserted anywhere in the life of the Apostle before the first Roman imprisonment. Hence the visit, as well as the composition of this Epistle, took place between St. Paul's liberation from this first imprisonment and his death. Catholic authors commonly hold that the Epistle was written shortly after the writing of 1 Timothy, in either A.D. 65 or 66.

The religious situation in Crete and the mission of Titus correspond to what confronted Timothy at Ephesus. Because of the character of the inhabitants and the spread of erroneous doctrines, Titus' task was a difficult one. Before leaving Titus at Crete, St. Paul had instructed him how to organize and rule the churches. In this Epistle the Apostle gives him counsels and instructions to guide him in his episcopal office.

The Epistle of St. Paul the Apostle to Titus

INTRODUCTION

Paul, a servant of God and apostle of Jesus Christ, in accordance with the faith of God's elect and the full knowledge of the truth which is according to piety, in the hope of life everlasting which God, who does not lie, promised before the ages began—he has in due times manifested his word through the preaching committed to my trust by the command of God our Savior—to Titus, my beloved son in the common faith: grace and peace from God the Father, and from Christ Jesus our Savior.

I. PASTORAL CHARGE

For this reason I left thee in Crete, that thou shouldst set right anything that is defective and shouldst appoint presbyters in every city, as I myself directed thee to do. They must be blameless, married but once, having believing children who are not accused of impurity or disobedience. For a bishop must be blameless as being the steward of God, not proud, or ill-tempered, or a drinker, or a brawler, or greedy for base gain; but hospitable, gentle, reserved, just, holy, continent; holding fast the faithful word which is in accordance with the teaching, that he may be able both to exhort in sound doctrine and to confute opponents.

For there are also many disobedient, vain babblers and deceivers, especially those of the circumcision. These must be rebuked, for they upset whole households, teaching things that they ought not, for the sake of base gain. One of themselves, a prophet of their own, said, "Cretans, always liars, evil beasts, lazy gluttons." This statement is true. Hence rebuke them sharply that they may be sound in faith, and may not listen to Jewish fables and the commandments of men who turn away from the truth. For the clean all things are clean, but for the defiled and unbelieving nothing is clean; for both their mind and their conscience are defiled. They profess to know God, but by their works they disown him, being abominable and unbelieving and worthless for any good work.

II. CHARGE TO TEACH THE CHRISTIAN LIFE

But do thou speak what befits the sound doctrine: that elderly men be reserved, honorable, prudent, sound in faith, in love, in patience; that elderly women, in like manner, be marked by holiness of behavior, not slanderers, nor enslaved to much wine; teaching what is right, that they may train the younger woman to be wise, to love their husbands and their children, to be discreet, chaste, domestic, gentle, obedient to their husbands, so that the word of God be not reviled. Exhort the younger men, in like manner, to be self-controlled. Show thyself in all things an example of good works, in teaching, in integrity and dignity; let thy speech be sound and blameless, so that anyone opposing may be put to shame, having nothing bad to say of us. Exhort slaves to obey their masters, pleasing them in all things and not opposing them; not pilfering, but showing faithfulness in all things, so as to adorn in all things the teaching of God our Savior.

For the grace of God our Savior has appeared to all men, instructing us, in order that, rejecting ungodliness and worldly lusts, we may live temperately and justly and piously in this world; looking for the blessed hope and glorious coming of our great God and Savior, Jesus Christ, who gave himself for us that he might redeem us from all iniquity and cleanse for himself an acceptable people, pursuing good works. Thus speak, and exhort, and rebuke, with all authority. Let no one despise thee.

Admonish them to be subject to princes and authorities, obeying commands, ready for every good work, speaking evil of none, not quarrelsome but moderate, showing all mildness to all men. For we ourselves also were once unwise, unbelieving, going astray, slaves to various lusts and pleasures, living in malice and envy, hateful and hating one another. But when the goodness and kindness of God our Savior appeared, then not by reason of good works that we did ourselves, but according to his mercy, he saved us through the bath of regeneration and renewal by the Holy Spirit; whom he has abundantly poured out upon us through Jesus Christ our Savior, in order that, justified by his grace, we may be heirs in the hope of life everlasting.

This saying is true, and concerning these things I desire thee to insist, that they who believe in God may be careful to excel in good works. These things are good and useful to men. But avoid foolish controversies and genealogies and quarrels and disputes about the Law; for they are useless and futile. A factious man avoid after a first and a second admonition, knowing that such a one is perverted and sins, being self-condemned.

CONCLUSION

When I send Artemas or Tychicus to thee, make every effort to come to me at Nicopolis; for there I have decided to spend the winter. Help Zenas the lawyer and Apollos on their way, taking care that nothing be wanting to them. And let our people also learn to excel in good works, in order to meet cases of necessity, that they may not be unfruitful.

All my companions greet thee. Greet those who love us in the faith. The grace of God be with you all. Amen.

A Note *about*
The Epistle of St. Paul the Apostle to Philemon

During his first Roman imprisonment (A.D. 60–63), St. Paul came to know a slave named Onesimus, who had deserted his master Philemon, a wealthy Christian of Colossae in Phrygia. After the Apostle had won the fugitive over to Christianity, he looked for a favorable opportunity to send him back to his master. This opportunity offered itself when he was dispatching a letter to the Colossians in A.D. 63. Onesimus accompanied St. Paul's messenger Tychicus (Colossians 4:7–9). To Philemon the Apostle addressed this touching appeal, entreating his friend to deal kindly with the runaway.

The Epistle of St. Paul the Apostle to Philemon

INTRODUCTION

Paul, a prisoner of Christ Jesus, and our brother Timothy, to Philemon, our beloved and fellow-worker, and to Appia, the sister, and to Archippus, our fellow-soldier, and to the church that is in thy house: grace be to you and peace from God our Father and from the Lord Jesus Christ.

I give thanks to my God, always making remembrance of thee in my prayers, as I hear of thy charity and of the faith that thou hast in our Lord Jesus and towards all the saints. May the sharing of thy faith be made evident in full knowledge of all the good that is in you, in Christ Jesus. For I had great joy and consolation in thy charity, because through thee, brother, the hearts of the saints have found rest.

For this reason, though I am very confident that I might charge thee in Christ Jesus to do what is fitting, yet for the sake of charity I prefer to plead, since thou art such as thou art; as Paul, an old man—and now also a prisoner of Jesus Christ—I plead with thee for my own son, whom I have begotten in prison, for Onesimus. He once was useless to thee, but now is useful both to me and to thee. I am sending him back to thee, and do thou welcome him as though he were my very heart. I had wanted to keep him here with me that in thy stead he might wait on me in my imprisonment for the gospel; but I did not want to do anything without thy counsel, in order that thy kindness might not be as it were of necessity, but voluntary.

Perhaps, indeed, he departed from thee for a short while so that thou mightest receive him forever, no longer as a slave, but instead of a slave as a brother most dear, especially to me, and how much more to thee, both in the flesh and in the Lord! If, therefore, thou dost count me as a partner, welcome him as thou wouldst me. And if he did thee any injury or owes thee anything, charge it to me. I, Paul, write it with my own hand: I will repay it—not to say to thee that thou owest me thy very self. Yes, indeed, brother! May I, too, make use of thee in the Lord! Console my heart in the Lord!

Trusting in thy compliance I am writing to thee, knowing that thou wilt do even beyond what I say. At the same time make ready a lodging for me too, for I hope that through your prayers I shall be restored to you. Epaphras, my fellow-prisoner in Christ Jesus, Mark, Aristarchus, Demas and Luke, my fellow-workers, send thee greetings. The grace of our Lord Jesus Christ be with your spirit. Amen.

A Note *about*
The Epistle of St. Paul the Apostle
to the Hebrews

Apart from some doubts expressed unofficially in the West before the fourth century, the traditional Catholic view has always maintained the Pauline authorship of the Epistle to the Hebrews at least in the sense that it was conceived by St. Paul and written under his direction. Its thought is thoroughly Pauline, and much of its phraseology is also distinctly Pauline. The excellent literary style, however, is generally superior to that found in the other Epistles of St. Paul, and it ranks with the best in the New Testament.

The time, place of composition, and destination of the Epistle are not stated explicitly, and there is but little evidence elsewhere bearing upon these matters. Opinions, based on the few vague indications available, differ widely. As plausible as any is the common view that the Epistle was written at Rome about A.D. 63, shortly after St. Paul's release from his first Roman imprisonment, and that it was destined for the Jewish Christians of Palestine, who under the stress of trials were in danger of relapsing into Judaism.

The Epistle describes most eloquently the eminent superiority of the new dispensation over the old. Inaugurated by the Son of God Himself, this new dispensation was God's final revelation to man. It completed the message of the prophets and brought to perfection all that was of permanent value in the Mosaic covenant. The Incarnate Son of God was its High Priest, and His glorious sacrifice was truly efficacious before God in the forgiveness of sin. As suffering and humiliation had an important place in His victory, His followers are exhorted to forego worldly advantage, to bear their trials patiently, and to persevere heroically in the faith.

The Epistle of St. Paul the Apostle to the Hebrews

I. SUPERIORITY OF THE NEW DISPENSATION OVER THE OLD

God, who at sundry times and in divers manners spoke in times past to the fathers by the prophets, last of all in these days has spoken to us by his Son, whom he appointed heir of all things, by whom also he made the world, who, being the brightness of his glory and the image of his substance, and upholding all things by the word of his power, has effected man's purgation from sin and taken his seat at the right hand of the Majesty on high, having become so much superior to the angels as he has inherited a more excellent name than they. For to which of the angels has he ever said, "Thou art my son, I this day have begotten thee"? And again, "I will be to him a father, and he shall be to me a son"? And again, when he brings the firstborn into the world, he says, "And let all the angels of God adore him." And of the angels indeed he says, "He makes his angels spirits, and his ministers a flame of fire." But of the Son, "Thy throne, O God, is forever and ever, and a sceptre of equity is the sceptre of thy kingdom. Thou hast loved justice and hated iniquity; therefore God, thy God, has anointed thee with the oil of gladness above thy fellows." And, "Thou in the beginning, O Lord, didst found the earth, and the heavens are works of thy hands. They shall perish, but thou shalt continue; and they shall all grow old as does a garment, and as a vesture shalt thou change them, and they shall be changed. But thou art the same, and thy years shall not fail." Now to which of the angels has he ever said, "Sit at my right hand, until I make thy enemies the footstool of thy feet"? Are they not all ministering spirits, sent for service, for the sake of those who shall inherit salvation?

Therefore ought we the more earnestly to observe the things that we have heard, lest perhaps we drift away. For if the word spoken by angels proved to be valid, and every transgression and disobedience received a just punishment, how shall we escape if we neglect so great a salvation? For it was first announced by the Lord and was confirmed unto us by those who heard him; God also, according to his own will, bearing them witness by signs and wonders, and by manifold powers, and by impartings of the Holy Spirit.

For he has not subjected to angels the world to come, whereof we speak. Rather someone has testified somewhere, saying, "What is man that thou art mindful of him, or the son of man that thou visitest him? Thou hast made him a little lower than the angels, thou hast crowned him with glory and honor, and hast set him over the works of thy hands; thou hast put all things under his feet." For in subjecting all things to man, he left nothing that is not subject to him. But now we do not see as yet all things subject to him. But we do see him who was made "a little lower than the angels," namely Jesus, crowned with glory and honor because of his having suffered death, that by the grace of God he might taste death for all. For it became him for whom are all things and through whom are all things, who had brought many sons into glory, to perfect through sufferings the author of their salvation. For both he who sanctifies and they who are sanctified are all from one. For which cause he is not ashamed to call them brethren, saying, "I will declare thy name to my brethren; in the midst of the church I will praise thee." And again, "I will put my trust in him." And again, "Behold, I and my children whom God has given me." Therefore because children have blood and flesh in common, so he in like manner has shared in these; that through death he might destroy him who had the empire of death, that is, the devil; and might deliver them, who throughout their life were kept in servitude by the fear of death. For, of course, it is not angels that he is succoring; but he is succoring the offspring of Abraham. Wherefore it was right that he should in all things be made like unto his brethren, that he might become a merciful and faithful high priest before God to expiate the sins of the people. For in that he himself suffered and has been tempted, he is able to help those who are tempted.

Therefore, holy brethren, partakers of a heavenly calling, consider the apostle and high priest of our confession, Jesus, who is faithful to him who made him, as was Moses also "in all his house." For he was deemed worthy of greater glory than Moses, just as the builder of a house has greater honor than the house that he has built. For every house is built by someone; but he who created all things is God. And Moses indeed was faithful "in all his house" as a servant, to testify concerning those things that were to be spoken; but Christ is faithful as the Son over his own house. We are that house, if we hold fast our confession and the hope in which we glory unto the end.

Therefore, as the Holy Spirit says, "Today if you shall hear his voice, do not harden your hearts as in the provocation, during the day of temptation in the desert, where your fathers tried me, proved and saw my works forty years. Wherefore I was offended with this generation, and said, 'They always err in heart, and they have not known my ways.' As I have sworn in my wrath, they shall not enter into my Rest." Take heed, brethren, lest perhaps there be in any of you an evil, unbelieving heart that would turn away from the living God. But exhort one another every day, while it is still Today, that none of you be hardened by the deceitfulness of sin. For we have been made partakers of Christ, provided only that we hold fast our first confidence in him unto the end. While it is said, "Today, if you shall hear his voice, do not harden your hearts as in that provocation"—for some who heard gave provocation, but not all those who came out of Egypt under Moses—with whom then was he offended forty years? Was it not with those who sinned, whose corpses fell in the desert? And to whom did he swear that they should not enter into his Rest, but to those who were unbelieving? And we see that they could not enter in because of unbelief.

Let us therefore fear lest perhaps, while the promise of entering into his Rest remains, any of you should be thought wanting. For to us also it has been declared, just as to them. But the word that was heard did not profit them, since they had no faith in what they heard. We then who have believed shall enter into his Rest, even as he said, "As I have sworn in my wrath, they shall not enter into my Rest." And indeed his works were completed at the foundation of the world. For somewhere he spoke of the seventh day thus, "And God rested the seventh day from all his works"; and in this place again, "They shall not enter into my Rest." Since then it follows that some are to enter into it, and they to whom it was first declared did not enter in because of unbelief, he again fixes another day to be Today, saying by David after so long a time, as quoted above, "Today if you shall hear his voice, do not harden your hearts." For if Josue had given them rest, God would never afterwards be speaking of another day. There remains therefore a Sabbath Rest for the people of God. For he who has entered into his Rest, has himself also rested from his own works, even as God did from his. Let us therefore hasten to enter into that Rest, lest anyone fall by following the same example of unbelief. For the word of God is living and efficient and keener than any two-edged sword, and extending even to the division of soul and spirit, of joints also and of marrow, and a discerner of the thoughts and intentions of the heart. And there is no creature hidden from his sight; but all things are naked and open to the eyes of him to whom we have to give account.

Having therefore a great high priest who has passed into the heavens, Jesus the Son of God, let us hold fast our confession. For we have not a high priest who cannot have compassion on our infirmities, but one tried as we are in all things except sin. Let us therefore draw near with confidence to the throne of grace, that we may obtain mercy and find grace to help in time of need.

For every high priest taken from among me is appointed

for men in the things pertaining to God, that he may offer gifts and sacrifices for sins. He is able to have compassion on the ignorant and erring, because he himself also is beset with weakness, and by reason thereof is obliged to offer for sins, as on behalf of the people, so also for himself. And no man takes the honor to himself; he takes it who is called by God, as Aaron was. So also Christ did not glorify himself with the high priesthood, but he who spoke to him, "Thou art my son, I this day have begotten thee." As he says also in another place, "Thou art a priest forever, according to the order of Melchisedech." For Jesus, in the days of his earthly life, with a loud cry and tears, offered up prayers and supplications to him who was able to save him from death, and was heard because of his reverent submission. And he, Son though he was, learned obedience from the things that he suffered; and when perfected, he became to all who obey him the cause of eternal salvation, called by God a high priest according to the order of Melchisedech.

On this point we have much to say, and it is difficult to explain it, because you have grown dull of hearing. For whereas by this time you ought to be masters, you need to be taught again the rudiments of the words of God; and you have become such as have need of milk and not of solid food. For everyone who is fed on milk is unskilled in the world of justice; he is but a child. But solid food is for the mature, for those who by practice have their faculties trained to discern good and evil.

Therefore, leaving the elementary teaching concerning Christ, let us pass on to things more perfect, not laying again a foundation of repentance from dead works and of faith towards God, of the doctrine of baptisms and the laying on of hands, of the resurrection of the dead and of eternal judgment. And this we will do, if God permits.

For it is impossible for those who were once enlightened, who have both tasted the heavenly gift and become partakers of the Holy Spirit, who have moreover tasted the good word of God and the powers of the world to come, and then have fallen away, to be renewed again to repentance; since they crucify again for themselves the Son of God and make him a mockery. For the earth that drinks in the rain that often falls upon it, and produces vegetation that is of use to those by whom it is tilled, receives a blessing from God; but that which brings forth thorns and thistles is worthless, and is nigh unto a curse, and its end is to be burnt.

But in your case, beloved, we are confident of better things, things that promise salvation, even though we speak thus. For God is not unjust, that he should forget your work and the love that you have shown in his name, you who have ministered and do minister to the saints. But we want every one of you to show to the very end the same earnestness for the fulfillment of your hopes; so that you may become not sluggish but imitators of those who by faith and patience will inherit the promises.

For when God made his promise to Abraham, since he had no greater to swear by, he swore by himself, saying, "I will surely bless thee, and I will surely multiply thee." And thus after patient waiting, Abraham obtained the promise. For men swear by one greater than themselves, and an oath given as a guarantee is the final settlement of all their disagreement. Hence God, meaning to show more abundantly to the heirs of the promise the unchangeableness of his will, interposed an oath, that by two unchangeable things, in which it is impossible for God to deceive, we may have the strongest comfort—we who have sought refuge in holding fast the hope set before us. This hope we have, as a sure and firm anchor of the soul, reaching even behind the veil where our forerunner Jesus has entered for us, having become a high priest forever according to the order of Melchisedech.

For this Melchisedech was king of Salem, priest of the most high God, who met Abraham returning from the slaughter of the kings and blessed him; to whom Abraham divided the tithes of all. First, as his name shows, he is King of justice, and then also he is King of Salem, that is, King of Peace. Without father, without mother, without genealogy, having neither beginning of days nor end of life, but likened to the Son of God, who continues a priest forever.

Now consider how great this man is, to whom even Abraham the patriarch gave tithes out of the best portions of the spoils. And indeed they who are of the priestly sons of Levi, have a commandment to take tithes from the people according to the Law, that is, from their brethren, though these also have come from the loins of Abraham. But he whose genealogy is not recorded among them received tithes of Abraham and blessed him who had the promises. Now beyond all contradiction, that which is less is blessed by the superior. And in the one case indeed, mortal men receive tithes, while in the other, it is one of whom it is testified that he lives on. And even Levi, the receiver of tithes, was also, so to speak, through Abraham made subject to tithes, for he was still in the loins of his father when Melchisedech met him.

If then perfection was by the Levitical priesthood (for under it the people received the Law), what further need was there that another priest should rise, according to the order of Melchisedech, and said not to be according to the order of Aaron? For when the priesthood is changed, it is necessary that a change of law be made also. For he of whom these things are said is from another tribe, from which no one has ever done service at the altar. For it is evident that our Lord has sprung out of Juda; and Moses spoke nothing at all about priests when referring to this tribe. And it is yet far more evident if there arise another priest, according to the likeness of Melchisedech, who has become so not according to the Law of carnal commandment, but according to a life that cannot end. For it is testified of him, "Thou art a priest forever, according to the order of Melchisedech."

On the one hand there is the rejection of the former commandment, because of its weakness and unprofitableness (for the Law brought nothing to perfection), and on the other hand a bringing in of a better hope, through which we draw near to God.

And inasmuch as it is not without an oath (for the others indeed were made priests without an oath, but he with an oath through him who said to him, "The Lord has sworn and will not repent, thou art a priest forever"), all the more has Jesus become surety of a superior covenant. And the other priests indeed were numerous, because they were prevented by death from continuing in office; but he, because he continues forever, has an everlasting priesthood. Therefore he is able at all times to save those who come to God through him, since he lives always to make intercession for them.

For it was fitting that we should have such a high priest, holy, innocent, undefiled, set apart from sinners, and become higher than the heavens. He does not need to offer sacrifices daily (as the other priests did), first for his own sins, and then for the sins of the people; for this latter he did once for all in offering up himself. For the Law appoints as priests men who are weak; but the word of the oath, which came after the Law, appoints a Son who is forever perfect.

Now the main point in what we are saying is this. We have such a high priest, who has taken his seat at the right hand of the throne of Majesty in the heavens, a minister of the Holies, and of the true tabernacle, which the Lord has erected and not man. For every high priest is appointed to offer gifts and sacrifices; therefore it is necessary that this one also should have something to offer. If then he were on earth, he would not even be a priest, since there are already others to offer gifts according to the Law. The worship they offer is a mere copy and shadow of things heavenly, even as Moses was warned when he was completing the tabernacle: "See," God said, "that thou make all things according to the pattern that was shown thee on the mount."

But now he has obtained a superior ministry, in proportion as he is mediator of a superior covenant, enacted on the basis of superior promises. For had the first been faultless, place would not of course be sought for a second. For finding fault with them he says, "Behold, days are coming, says the Lord, when I will make a new covenant with the house of Israel and with the house of Juda, not according to the covenant that I made with their fathers on the day when I took them by the hand to lead them forth out of the land of Egypt; for they did not abide by my covenant, and I did not regard them, says the Lord. For this is the covenant that I will make with the house of Israel after those days, says the Lord: I will put my laws into their minds, and upon their hearts I will write them, and I will be their God, and they shall be my people. And they shall not teach, each his neighbor, and each his brother, saying, 'Know the Lord'; for all shall know me, from least to greatest among them. Because I will be merciful to their iniquities, and their sins I will remember no more." Now in saying, "a new covenant," he has made obsolete the former one; and that which is obsolete and has grown old is near its end.

The first covenant also had ritual ordinances and a sanctuary, though an earthly one. For there was set up a tabernacle in the outer part of which were the lamp-stand and the table and the showbread, and this is called the Holy Place; but beyond the second veil was the tabernacle which is called the Holy of Holies, having a golden censer and the ark of the covenant, overlaid on every side with gold. In the ark was a golden pot containing the manna and the rod of Aaron which had budded, and the tablets of the covenant; and above it were the cherubim of glory overshadowing the mercy-seat. But of all these we cannot now speak in detail.

Such then being the arrangements, the priests always used to enter into the first tabernacle to perform the sacred rites; but into the second tabernacle the high priest alone entered once a year, not without blood, which he offered for his own and the people's sins of ignorance. The Holy Spirit signified by this that the way into the Holies was not yet thrown open while the first tabernacle was still standing. The first tabernacle is a figure of the present time, inasmuch as gifts and sacrifices are offered that cannot perfect the worshipper in conscience, since they refer only to food and drink and various ablutions and bodily regulations imposed until a time of reformation.

But when Christ appeared as high priest of the good things to come, he entered once for all through the greater and more perfect tabernacle, not made by hands (that is, not of this creation), nor again by virtue of blood of goats and calves, but by virtue of his own blood, into the Holies, having obtained eternal redemption. For if the blood of goats and bulls and the sprinkled ashes of a heifer sanctify the unclean unto the cleansing of the flesh, how much more will the blood of Christ, who through the Holy Spirit offered himself unblemished unto God, cleanse your conscience from dead works to serve the living God?

And this is why he is mediator of a new covenant, that whereas a death has taken place for redemption from the transgressions committed under the former covenant, they who have been called may receive eternal inheritance according to the promise. For where there is a testament, the death of the testator must intervene; for a testament is valid only when men are dead, otherwise it has as yet no force as long as the testator is alive.

Hence not even the first has been inaugurated without blood; for when every commandment of the Law had been read by Moses to all the people, he took the blood of the calves and of the goats, with water and scarlet wool and hyssop, and sprinkled both the book itself and all the people, saying, "This is the blood of the covenant which God has commanded for you." The tabernacle also and all the vessels of the ministry he sprinkled likewise with blood; and with blood almost everything is cleansed according to the Law, and without the shedding of blood there is no forgiveness.

It was necessary, therefore, that the copies of the heavenly realities should be cleansed by these things; but the heavenly realities themselves require better sacrifices than these. For Jesus has not entered into a Holies made by hands, a mere copy of the true, but into heaven itself, to appear now before the face of God on our behalf; nor yet has he entered to offer himself often, as the high priest enters into the Holies year after year with blood not his own; for in that case he must have suffered often since the beginning of the world. But as it is, once for all at the end of the ages, he has appeared for the destruction of sin by the sacrifice of himself. And just as it is appointed unto men to die once and after this comes the judgment, so also was Christ offered once to take away the sins of many; the second time with no part in sin he will appear unto the salvation of those who await him.

For the Law, having but a shadow of the good things to come, and not the exact image of the objects, is never able by the sacrifices which they offer continually, year after year the same, to perfect those who draw near; for in that case would they not have ceased to be offered, because the worshippers, once cleansed, would no longer have any consciousness of sin? Yet in these sacrifices sins are brought to remembrance year by year. For it is impossible that sins should be taken away with blood of bulls and of goats. Therefore in coming into the world, he says, "Sacrifice and oblation thou wouldst not, but a body thou hast fitted to me: In holocausts and sin-offerings thou hast had no pleasure. Then said I, 'Behold, I come—(in the head of the book it is written of me)—to do thy will, O God.'" In saying in the first place, "Sacrifices and oblations and holocausts and sin-offerings thou wouldst not, neither hast thou had pleasure in them" (which are offered according to the Law), and then saying, "Behold, I come to do thy will, O God," he annuls the first covenant in order to establish the second. It is in this "will" that we have been sanctified through the offering of the body of Jesus Christ once for all.

And every priest indeed stands daily ministering, and often offering the same sacrifices, which can never take away sins; but Jesus, having offered one sacrifice for sins, has taken his seat forever at the right hand of God, waiting thenceforth until his enemies be made the footstool under his feet. For by one offering he has perfected forever those who are sanctified. Thus also the Holy Spirit testifies unto us. For after having said, "This is the covenant that I will make with them after those days, says the Lord: I will put my laws upon their hearts, and upon their minds I will write them," he then adds, "And their sins and their iniquities I will remember no more." Now where there is forgiveness of sins, there is no longer offering for sin.

II. EXHORTATIONS

Since then, brethren, we are free to enter the Holies in virtue of the blood of Christ, a new and living way which he inaugurated for us through the veil (that is, his flesh), and since we have a high priest over the house of God, let us draw near with a true heart in fullness of faith, having our hearts cleansed from an evil conscience by sprinkling, and the body washed with clean water. Let us hold fast the confession of our hope without wavering, for he who has given the promise is faithful. And let us consider how to arouse one another to charity and good works; not forsaking our assembly as is the custom of some, but exhorting one another, and this all the more as you see the Day drawing near.

For if we sin willfully after receiving the knowledge of the truth, there remains no longer a sacrifice for sins, but a certain dreadful expectation of judgment, and "the fury of a fire which will consume the adversaries." A man making void the Law of Moses dies without any mercy on the word of two or three witnesses; how much worse punishments do you think he deserves who has trodden under foot the Son of God, and has regarded as unclean the blood of the covenant through which he was sanctified, and has insulted the Spirit of grace? For we know him who has said, "Vengeance is mine, I will repay." And again, "The Lord will judge his people." It is a fearful thing to fall into the hands of the living God.

But call to mind the days gone by, in which, after you had been enlightened, you endured a great conflict of sufferings; partly by being made a public spectacle through reproaches and tribulations, and partly by making common cause with those who fared thus. For you both have had compassion on those in prison and have joyfully accepted the plundering of your own goods, knowing that you have a better possession and a lasting one. Do not, therefore, lose your confidence, which has a great reward. For you have need of patience that, doing the will of God, you may receive the promise: "For yet a very little while, and he who is to come, will come, and will not delay. Now my just one lives by faith. But if he draws back, he will not please my soul." We, however, are not of those who draw back unto destruction, but of those who have faith to the saving of the soul.

Now faith is the substance of things to be hoped for, the evidence of things that are not seen; for by it the men of old had testimony borne to them. By faith we understand that the world was fashioned by the word of God; and thus things visible were made out of things invisible.

By faith Abel offered to God a sacrifice more excellent than did Cain, through which he obtained a testimony that he was just, God giving testimony to his gifts; and through his faith, though he is dead, he yet speaks.

By faith Henoch was taken up lest he should see death; and he was not found, because God took him up. For before he was taken up he had testimony that he pleased God, and without faith it is impossible to please God. For he who comes to God must believe that God exists and is a rewarder to those who seek him.

By faith Noe, having been warned concerning things not seen as yet, prepared with pious fear an ark in which to save his household. Having thus condemned the world, he was made heir of the justice which is through faith.

By faith he who is called Abraham obeyed by going out into a place which he was to receive for an inheritance; and he went out, not knowing where he was going. By faith he abode in the Land of Promise as in a foreign land, dwelling in tents with Isaac and Jacob, the co-heirs of the same promise; for he was looking for the city with fixed foundations, of which city the architect and the builder is God.

By faith even Sara herself, who was barren, received power for the conception of a child when she was past the time of life, because she believed that he who had given the promise was faithful. And so there sprang from one man, though he was as good as dead, issue like the stars of heaven in number and innumerable as the sand that is by the seashore.

In the way of faith all these died without receiving the promises, but beholding them afar off, and saluting them and acknowledging that they were pilgrims and strangers on earth. For they who say these things show plainly that they seek a country of their own. And indeed if they were thinking of the country from which they went out, they certainly would have had opportunity to return; but as it is they seek after a better, that is, a heavenly country. Therefore God is not ashamed to be called their God, for he has prepared for them a city.

By faith Abraham, when he was put to the test, offered Isaac; and he who had received the promises (to whom it had been said, "In Isaac thy seed shall be called") was about to offer up his only-begotten son, reasoning that God has power to raise up even from the dead; whence also he received him back as a type.

By faith Isaac blessed Jacob and Esau even regarding things to come. By faith Jacob, when dying, blessed each of the sons of Joseph and bowed in worship towards the top of his staff. By faith Joseph, when dying, made mention of the departure of the sons of Israel and gave orders concerning his bones.

By faith Moses was hidden by his parents for three months after his birth, because they saw he was a beautiful babe and they did not fear the king's edict.

By faith Moses, when he was grown up, denied that he was a son of Pharaoh's daughter; choosing rather to be afflicted with the people of God than to have the enjoyment of sin for a time, esteeming the reproach of Christ greater riches than the treasures of the Egyptians; for he was look-ing to the reward. By faith he left Egypt, not fearing the wrath of the king; for he persevered as if seeing him who cannot be seen. By faith he celebrated the Passover and the sprinkling of blood, that he who destroyed the firstborn might not touch them.

By faith they passed through the Red Sea, as through dry land; whereas the Egyptians, attempting it, were swallowed up. By faith the walls of Jericho fell after they had gone around them for seven days.

By faith Rahab the harlot, who had received the spies in peace, did not perish with the unbelievers.

And what more shall I say? For time will fail me if I tell of Gideon, of Barac, of Samson, of Jephthe, of David and of Samuel and the prophets, who by faith conquered kingdoms, wrought justice, obtained promises, stopped the mouths of lions, quenched the violence of fire, escaped the edge of the sword, recovered strength from weakness, became valiant in battle, put to flight armies of aliens. Women had their dead re-stored to them by resurrection. Others were tortured, refusing to accept release, that they might find a better resurrection. Others had experience of mockery and stripes, yes, even of chains and prisons. They were stoned, they were sawed asun-der, they were tempted, they were put to death by the sword. They went about in sheepskins and goatskins, destitute, dis-tressed, afflicted—of whom the world was not worthy—wan-dering in deserts, mountains, caves and holes in the earth.

And all these, though they had been approved by the testimony of faith, did not receive what was promised, for God had something better in view for us; so that they should not be perfected without us.

Therefore let us also, having such a cloud of witnesses over us, put away every encumbrance and the sin entangling us, and run with patience to the fight set before us; looking towards the author and finisher of faith, Jesus, who for the joy set before him, endured a cross, despising shame, and sits at the right hand of the throne of God. Consider, then, him who endured such opposition from sinners against himself, so that you may not grow weary and lose heart.

For you have not yet resisted unto blood in the struggle with sin. And you have forgotten the exhortation that is addressed to you as sons, saying, "My son, neglect not the discipline of the Lord, neither be thou weary when thou art rebuked by him. For whom the Lord loves, he chastises; and he scourges every son whom he receives."

Continue under discipline. God deals with us as with sons; for what son is there whom his father does not correct? But if you are without discipline, in which all have had a share, then you are illegitimate children and not sons. Furthermore, we had fathers of our flesh to correct us, and we reverenced them. Shall we not much more obey the Father of spirits and live? For they indeed corrected us for a few days, as they saw fit; but he for our benefit, that we may share his holiness. Now all discipline seems for the present to be a matter not for joy but for grief; but afterwards it yields the most peaceful fruit of justice to those who have been exercised by it. Therefore brace up the hands that hang down, and the tottering knees, and make straight paths for your feet; that no one who is lame may go out of the way, but rather be healed.

Strive for peace with all men, and for that holiness without which no man will see God. Take heed lest anyone be wanting in the grace of God; lest any root of bitterness springing up cause trouble and by it the many be defiled; lest there be any immoral or profane person, such as Esau, who for one meal sold his birthright. For know that even afterwards, when he desired to inherit the blessing, he was rejected; for he found no opportunity for repentance, although he had sought after it with tears.

For you have not approached a mountain that may be touched, and a burning fire, and whirlwind and darkness and storm, and sound of trumpet, and sound of words; which sound was such that those who heard entreated that the word should not be spoken to them; for they could not bear what was being said: "And if even a beast touches the mount, it shall be stoned." And so terrible was the spectacle that Moses said, "I am greatly terrified and trembling." But you have come to Mount Sion, and to the city of the living God, the heavenly Jerusalem, and to the company of many thousands of angels, and to the Church of the firstborn who are enrolled in the heavens, and to God, the judge of all, and to the spirits of the just made perfect, and to Jesus, mediator of a new covenant, and to a sprinkling of blood which speaks better than Abel. See that you do not refuse him who speaks. For if they did not escape who rejected him who spoke upon earth, much more shall we not escape who turn away from him who speaks to us from heaven. His voice then shook the earth, but now he promises thus, "Yet once, and I will shake not the earth only but heaven also." Now by this expression, "yet once," he announces the removal of things which can be shaken—created things—in order that the things which cannot be shaken may remain. Therefore, since we receive a kingdom that cannot be shaken, we have grace, through which we may offer pleasing service to God with fear and reverence. For our God is a consuming fire.

Let brotherly love abide in you, and do not forget to entertain strangers; for thereby some have entertained angels unawares. Remember those who are in bonds as if you were bound with them, and those who are ill-treated, as tarrying yourselves also in the body. Let marriage be held in honor with all, and let the marriage bed be undefiled. For God will judge the immoral and adulterers.

Let your manner of life be without avarice; be content with what you have, for he himself has said, "I will not leave thee, neither will I forsake thee." So that we may confidently say, "The Lord is my helper: I will not fear what man shall do to me."

Remember your superiors, who spoke to you the word of God. Consider how they ended their lives, and imitate their faith. Jesus Christ is the same, yesterday and today, yes, and forever.

Do not be led away by various and strange doctrines. For it is good to make steadfast the heart by grace, not by foods, in which those who walked found no profit. We have an altar, from which they have no right to eat who serve the tabernacle. For the bodies of those animals whose blood is brought into the Holies by the high priest for sin, are burned outside the camp; and so Jesus also, that he might sanctify the people by his blood, suffered outside the gate. Let us therefore go forth to him outside the camp, bearing his reproach; for here we have no permanent city, but we seek for the city that is to come. Through him, therefore, let us offer up a sacrifice of praise always to God, that is, fruit of lips praising his name. And do not forget kindness and charity, for by such sacrifices God's favor is obtained. Obey your superiors and be subject to them, for they keep watch as having to render an account of your souls; so that they may do this with joy, and not with grief, for that would not be expedient for you.

CONCLUSION

Pray for us. For we are confident that we have a good conscience, desiring to live uprightly in all things. But I more especially exhort you to do this, that I may be restored to you the sooner.

Now may the God of peace, who brought forth from the dead the great pastor of the sheep, our Lord Jesus, in virtue of the blood of an everlasting covenant, fit you with every good thing to do his will; working in you that which is well pleasing in his sight, through Jesus Christ, to whom is glory forever and ever. Amen.

And I beseech you, brethren, to bear with this word of exhortation; for I have written to you in few words. Know that our brother Timothy has been set free; with whom (if he comes soon) I will see you. Greet all your superiors and all the saints. The brethren from Italy send you greetings. Grace be with you all. Amen.

A Note *about*
The Epistle of St. James the Apostle

St. James the Less was the son of Alpheus or Cleophas. His mother Mary was a sister, or a close relative, of the Blessed Virgin, and for that reason, according to Jewish custom, he was sometimes called the brother of the Lord. According to tradition, he was the first Bishop of Jerusalem and was at the Council of Jerusalem about the year 50. The historians Eusebius and Hegesippus relate that St. James was martyred for the faith in the spring of the year 62.

Internal evidence based on the language, style, and teaching of the Epistle reveals its author as a Jew familiar with the Old Testament—and a Christian thoroughly grounded in the teachings of the gospel. External evidence from the early Fathers and councils of the Church confirms its authenticity and canonicity.

The date of its writing cannot be determined exactly. According to some scholars it was written about the year 49. Others, however, claim it was written after St. Paul's Epistle to the Romans (composed during the winter of 57–58). It was probably written between the years 60 and 62.

St. James addresses himself to Christians outside Palestine;

but nothing in the Epistle indicates that he is thinking only of Jewish Christians. St. James realizes full well the temptations and difficulties they encounter in the midst of paganism, and as a spiritual father, he endeavers to guide and direct them in the faith. Therefore the burden of his discourse is an exhortation to practical Christian living.

The Epistle of St. James the Apostle

INTRODUCTION

James, the servant of God and of our Lord Jesus Christ, to the twelve tribes that are in the Dispersion: greeting.

I. EXHORTATION TO PATIENCE IN TRIALS

Esteem it all joy, my brethren, when you fall into various trials, knowing that the trying of your faith begets patience. And let patience have its perfect work, that you may be perfect and entire, lacking nothing.

But if any of you is wanting in wisdom, let him ask it of God, who gives abundantly to all men, and does not reproach; and it will be given to him. But let him ask with faith, without hesitation. For he who hesitates is like a wave of the sea, driven and carried about by the wind. Therefore, let not such a one think that he will receive anything from the Lord, being a double-minded man, unstable in all his ways.

But let the brother of lowly condition glory in his high estate, and the rich man in his low condition; for he will pass away like the flower of the grass. For the sun rises with a burning heat and parches the grass, and its flower falls and the beauty of its appearance perishes. So too will the rich man wither in his ways.

Blessed is the man who endures temptation; for when he has been tried, he will receive the crown of life which God has promised to those who love him.

Let no man say when he is tempted, that he is tempted by God; for God is no tempter to evil, and he himself tempts no one. But everyone is tempted by being drawn away and enticed by his own passion. Then when passion has conceived, it brings forth sin; but when sin has matured, it begets death. Therefore, my beloved brethren, do not err.

Every good gift and every perfect gift is from above, coming down from the Father of Lights, with whom there is no change, nor shadow of alteration. Of his own will he has begotten us by the word of truth, that we might be, as it were, the first-fruits of his creatures.

II. LIVING AND ACTIVE FAITH

You know this, my beloved brethren. But let every man be swift to hear, slow to speak, and slow to wrath. For the wrath of man does not work the justice of God. Therefore, casting aside all uncleanness and abundance of malice, with meekness receive the ingrafted word, which is able to save your souls. But be doers of the word, and not hearers only, deceiving yourselves. For if anyone is a hearer of the word, and not a doer, he is like a man looking at his natural face in a mirror: for he looks at himself and goes away, and presently he forgets what kind of man he is. But he who has looked carefully into the perfect law of liberty and has remained in it, not becoming a forgetful hearer but a doer of the work, shall be blessed in his deed. And if anyone thinks himself to be religious, not restraining his tongue but deceiving his own heart, that man's religion is vain. Religion pure and undefiled before God the Father is this: to give aid to orphans and widows in their tribulation, and to keep oneself unspotted from this world.

My brethren, do not join faith in our glorious Lord Jesus Christ with partiality towards persons. For if a man in fine apparel, having a gold ring, enters your assembly, and a poor man in mean attire enters also, and you pay attention to him who is clothed in fine apparel and say, "Sit thou here in this good place"; but you say to the poor man, "Stand thou there," or, "Sit by my footstool"; are you not making distinctions among yourselves, and do not you become judges with evil thoughts? Listen, my beloved brethren! Has not God chosen the poor of this world to be rich in faith and heirs of the kingdom which God has promised to those who love him? But you have dishonored the poor man. Do not the rich use their power to oppress you, and do they not drag you before judgment-seats? Do they not blaspheme the good name by which you are called?

If, however, you fulfill the royal law, according to the Scriptures, "Thou shalt love thy neighbor as thyself," you do well. But if you show partiality towards persons, you commit sin, being convicted by the law as transgressors. For whoever keeps the whole law, but offends in one point, has become guilty in all. For he who said, "Thou shalt not commit adultery," said also, "Thou shalt not kill." Now if thou wilt not commit adultery, yet wilt commit murder, thou hast become a transgressor of the law. So speak and so act as men about to be judged by the law of liberty. For judgment is without mercy to him who has not shown mercy; but mercy triumphs over judgment.

What will it profit, my brethren, if a man says he has faith, but does not have works? Can the faith save him? And if a brother or a sister be naked and in want of daily food, and one of you say to them, "Go in peace, be warmed and filled," yet you do not give them what is necessary for the body, what does it profit? So faith too, unless it has works, is dead in itself. But someone will say, "Thou hast faith, and I have works." Show me thy faith without works, and I from my works will show thee my faith. Thou believest that there is one God. Thou dost well. The devils also believe, and tremble.

But dost thou want to know, O senseless man, that faith without works is useless? Was not Abraham our father justified by works, when he offered up Isaac his son upon the altar? Dost thou see that faith worked along with his works, and by the works the faith was made perfect? And the Scripture was fulfilled which says, "Abraham believed God, and it was reckoned to him as justice, and he was called the friend of God." You see that by works a man is justified, and not by faith only. In like manner, was not Rahab the harlot also justified by works, when she welcomed the messengers and sent them out another way? For just as the body without the spirit is dead, so faith also without works is dead.

III. THE HAZARD OF TEACHING

Let not many of you become teachers, my brethren, knowing that you will receive a greater judgment. For in many things we all offend. If anyone does not offend in word, he is a perfect man, able also to lead round by a bridle the whole body. For if we put bits into horses' mouths that they may obey us, we control their whole body also. Behold, even the ships, great as they are, and driven by boisterous winds, are steered by a small rudder wherever the touch of the steersman pleases. So the tongue also is a little member, but it boasts mightily. Behold, how small a fire—how great a forest it kindles! And the tongue is a fire, the very world of iniquity. The tongue is placed among our members, defiling the whole body, and setting on fire the course of our life, being itself set on fire by hell. For every kind of beast and bird, and of serpents and the rest, is tamed and has been tamed by mankind; but the tongue no man can tame—a restless evil, full of deadly poison. With it we bless God the Father; and with it we curse men, who have been made after the likeness of God. Out of the same mouth proceed blessing and cursing. These things, my brethren, ought not to be so. Does the fountain send forth sweet and bitter water from the same opening? Can a fig tree, my brethren, bear olives, or a vine figs? So neither can salt water yield fresh water.

Who is wise and instructed among you? Let him by his good behavior show his work in the meekness of wisdom. But if you have bitter jealousy and contentions in your hearts, do not glory and be liars against the truth. This is not the wisdom that descends from above. It is earthly, sensual, devilish. For where there is envy and contentiousness, there is instability and every wicked deed. But the wisdom that is from above is first of all chaste, then peaceable, moderate, docile, in harmony with good things, full of mercy and good fruits, without judging, without dissimulation. The fruit of justice is sown in peace by those who make peace.

IV. SPECIAL ADMONITIONS

Whence do wars and quarrels come among you? Is it not from this, from your passions, which wage war in your members? You covet and do not have; you kill and envy, and cannot obtain. You quarrel and wrangle, and you do not have because you do not ask. You ask and do not receive, because you ask amiss, that you may spend it upon your passions. Adulterers, do you not know that the friendship of this world is enmity with God? Therefore, whoever wishes to be a friend of this world becomes an enemy of God. Or do you think that the Scripture says in vain, "The Spirit which dwells in you covets unto jealousy"? But he gives a greater grace. For this reason it says, "God resists the proud, but gives grace to the humble." Be subject therefore to God, but resist the devil, and he will flee from you. Draw near to God, and he will draw near to you. Cleanse your hands, you sinners, and purify your hearts, you double-minded. Be sorrowful, and mourn, and weep; let your laughter be turned into mourning, and your joy into sadness. Humble yourselves in the sight of the Lord, and he will exalt you.

Brethren, do not speak against one another. He who speaks against a brother, or judges his brother, speaks against the law and judges the law. But if thou judgest the law, thou art not a doer of the law, but a judge. There is one Lawgiver and Judge, he who is able to destroy and to save. But thou who judgest thy neighbor, who art thou?

Behold now, you who say, "Today or tomorrow we will go into such a city, and spend a year there, and trade and make money"; you who do not know what will happen tomorrow. For what is your life? It is a mist that appears for a little while, and then vanishes. You ought rather to say, "If the Lord will," and, "If we live, we will do this or that." But now you boast in your arrogance. All such boasting is evil. Therefore he who knows how to do good, and does not do it, commits a sin.

Come now, you rich, weep and howl over your miseries which will come upon you. Your riches have rotted and your garments have become moth-eaten. Your gold and silver are rusted; and their rust will be a witness against you, and will devour your flesh as fire does. You have laid up treasure in the last days. Behold, the wages of the laborers who reaped your fields, which have been kept back by you unjustly, cry out; and their cry has entered into the ears of the Lord of Hosts. You have feasted upon earth, and you have nourished your hearts on dissipation in the day of slaughter. You have condemned and put to death the just, and he did not resist you.

CONCLUSION

Be patient, therefore, brethren, until the coming of the Lord. Behold, the farmer waits for the precious fruit of the earth, being patient until it receives the early and the late rain. Do you also be patient; strengthen your hearts; for the coming of the Lord is at hand. Do not complain against one another, brethren, that you may not be judged. Behold, the judge is standing at the door. Take, brethren, as an example of labor and patience, the prophets who spoke in the name of the Lord. Behold, we call them blessed who have endured. You have heard of the patience of Job, and you have seen the purpose of the Lord, how the Lord is merciful and compassionate. But above all things, brethren, do not swear, either by heaven or by the earth, or any other oath; but let your yes be yes, your no, no; that you may not fall under judgment.

Is any one of you sad? Let him pray. Is any one in good spirits? Let him sing a hymn. Is any one among you sick? Let him bring in the presbyters of the Church, and let them pray over him, anointing him with oil in the name of the Lord. And the prayer of faith will save the sick man, and the Lord will raise him up, and if he be in sins, they shall be forgiven him. Confess, therefore, your sins to one another, and pray for one another, that you may be saved. For the unceasing prayer of a just man is of great avail. Elias was a man like ourselves, subject to the same infirmities; and he prayed earnestly that it might not rain upon the earth, and it did not rain for three years and six months. He prayed again, and the heavens gave rain and the earth brought forth its fruit.

My brethren, if any one of you strays from the truth and someone brings him back, he ought to know that he who causes a sinner to be brought back from his misguided way, will save his soul from death, and will cover a multitude of sins.

A Note about
The First Epistle of St. Peter the Apostle

St. Peter was led by his brother Andrew to the Lord, who conferred upon him the name Cephas, i.e., "rock" or Peter. After the Resurrection the primacy was conferred upon him, and immediately after the Ascension he began to exercise it. After preaching in Jerusalem and Palestine he went to Rome, probably after his liberation from prison. Some years later he was in Jerusalem for the first Church Council—and shortly afterwards at Antioch. In A.D. 67 he was martyred in Rome.

The Epistle names St. Peter, Apostle of Jesus Christ, as its author, and the testimony of the early centuries of Christianity reaffirms this evidence. Its authorship is also confirmed by the contents of the Epistle, in which the author appears as an immediate witness of the sufferings of Christ, and by its similarity to St. Peter's discourses in Acts.

The Epistle is addressed to the Christian communities of Asia Minor that were being distressed by the enmity of their pagan neighbors. By their acceptance of Christianity they had become separated from their own countrymen, who abused and persecuted them. The Apostle therefore instructs his readers that Christianity is the true religion in spite of their trials and sufferings, and he exhorts them to lead good Christian lives.

The place of composition is given as "Babylon" (5:13). We know that this name was a cryptic designation of the city of Rome. Since the author seems to be familiar with the Epistle to the Ephesians, which was written in A.D. 63, and since he makes no reference to the persecution of Nero, which began about the end of A.D. 64, it appears very likely that the letter was written in the latter part of 63 or the beginning of 64.

The First Epistle of St. Peter the Apostle

INTRODUCTION

Peter, an apostle of Jesus Christ, to the sojourners of the Dispersion in Pontus, Galatia, Cappadocia, Asia and Bithynia, chosen unto the sanctification of the Spirit according to the foreknowledge of God the Father, unto obedience to Jesus Christ and the sprinkling of his blood: grace and peace be given you in abundance.

Blessed be the God and Father of our Lord Jesus Christ, who according to his great mercy has begotten us again, through the resurrection of Jesus Christ from the dead, unto a living hope, unto an incorruptible inheritance—undefiled and unfading, reserved for you in heaven. By the power of God you are guarded through faith for salvation, which is ready to be revealed in the last time. Over this you rejoice; though now for a little while, if need be, you are made sorrowful by various trials, that the temper of your faith—more precious by far than gold which is tried by fire—may be found unto praise and glory and honor at the revelation of Jesus Christ. Him, though you have not seen, you love.

In him, though you do not see him, yet believing, you exult with a joy unspeakable and triumphant; receiving, as the final issue of your faith, the salvation of your souls. The prophets who foretold the grace that was to come for you made earnest inquiry and search concerning this salvation. They searched what time or circumstances the Spirit of Christ in them was signifying, when he foretold the sufferings of Christ, and the glories that would follow. To them it was revealed that not to themselves but to you they were ministering those things which now have been declared to you by those who preached the gospel to you by the Holy Spirit sent from heaven. Into these things angels desire to look.

I. GENERAL COUNSELS OF CHRISTIAN HOLINESS

Therefore, having girded up the loins of your understanding, be sober and set your hope completely upon that grace which is brought to you in the revelation of Jesus Christ. As obedient children, do not conform to the lusts of former days when you were ignorant; but as the One who called you is holy, be you also holy in all your behavior; for it is written, "You shall be holy, because I am holy."

And if you invoke as Father him who without respect of persons judges according to each one's work, conduct yourselves with fear in the time of your sojourning. You know that you were redeemed from the vain manner of life handed down from your fathers, not with perishable things, with silver or gold, but with the precious blood of Christ, as of a lamb without blemish and without spot. Foreknown, indeed, before the foundation of the world, he has been manifested in the last times for your sakes. Through him you are believers in God who raised him up from the dead and gave him glory, so that your faith and hope might be in God.

Now that your obedience to charity has purified your souls for a brotherly love that is sincere, love one another heartily and intensely. For you have been reborn, not from corruptible seed but from incorruptible, through the word of God who lives and abides forever. For, "All flesh is as grass, and all its glory as the flower of grass; the grass withered, and the flower has fallen—but the word of the Lord endures forever." Now this is the word of the gospel that was preached to you.

Lay aside therefore all malice, and all deceit, and pretense, and envy, and all slander. Crave, as newborn babes, pure spiritual milk, that by it you may grow to salvation; if, indeed, you have tasted that the Lord is sweet. Draw near to him, a living stone, rejected indeed by men but chosen and honored by God. Be you yourselves as living stones, built thereon into a spiritual house, a holy priesthood, to offer spiritual sacrifices acceptable to God through Jesus Christ. Hence Scripture says, "Behold, I lay in Sion a chief cornerstone, chosen, precious; and he who believes in it shall not be put to shame." For you, therefore, who believe is this honor; but to those who do not believe, "A stone which the builders rejected, the same has become the head of the corner," and, "A stumbling-stone, and a rock of scandal," to those who stumble at the word, and who do not believe. For this also they are destined. You, however, are a chosen race, a royal priesthood, a holy nation, a purchased people;

that you may proclaim the perfections of him who has called you out of darkness into his marvellous light. You who in times past were not a people, but are now the people of God; who had not obtained mercy, but now have obtained mercy.

II. PARTICULAR COUNSELS OF CHRISTIAN CONDUCT

Beloved, I exhort you as strangers and pilgrims to abstain from carnal desires which war against the soul. Behave yourselves honorably among the pagans; that, whereas they slander you as evildoers, they may, through observing you, by reason of your good works glorify God in the day of visitation.

Be subject to every human creature for God's sake, whether to the king as supreme, or to governors as sent through him for vengeance on evildoers and for the praise of the good. For such is the will of God, that by doing good you should put to silence the ignorance of foolish men. Live as freemen, yet not using your freedom as a cloak for malice but as servants of God. Honor all men; love the brotherhood; fear God; honor the king.

Servants, be subject to your masters in all fear, not only to the good and moderate, but also to the severe. This is indeed a grace, if for consciousness of God anyone endure sorrows, suffering unjustly. For what is the glory if, when you sin and are buffeted, you endure it? But if, when you do right and suffer, you take it patiently, this is acceptable with God. Unto this, indeed, you have been called, because Christ also has suffered for you, leaving you an example that you may follow in his steps: "Who did no sin, neither was deceit found in his mouth." Who, when he was reviled, did not revile, when he suffered, did not threaten, but yielded himself to him who judged him unjustly; who himself bore our sins in his body upon the tree, that we, having died to sin, might live to justice; and by his stripes you were healed. For you were as sheep going astray, but now you have returned to the shepherd and guardian of your souls.

In like manner also let wives be subject to their husbands; so that even if any do not believe the word, they may without word be won through the behavior of their wives, observing reverently your chaste behavior. Let not theirs be the outward adornment of braiding the hair, or of wearing gold, or of putting on robes; but let it be the inner life of the heart, in the imperishableness of a quiet and gentle spirit, which is of great price in the sight of God. For after this manner in old times the holy women also who hoped in God adorned themselves, while being subject to their husbands. So Sara obeyed Abraham, calling him lord. You are daughters of hers when you do what is right and fear no disturbance.

Husbands, in like manner dwell with your wives considerately, paying honor to the woman as to the weaker vessel, and as co-heir of the grace of life, that your prayers be not hindered.

Finally, be all like-minded, compassionate, lovers of the brethren, merciful, humble; not rendering evil for evil, or abuse for abuse, but contrariwise, blessing; for unto this were you called that you might inherit a blessing. For, "He who would love life, and see good days, let him refrain his tongue from evil, and his lips that they speak no deceit. Let him turn away from evil and do good, let him seek after peace and pursue it. For the eyes of the Lord are upon the just, and his ears unto their prayers; but the face of the Lord is against those who do evil."

And who is there to harm you, if you are zealous for what is good? But even if you suffer anything for justice' sake, blessed are you. So have no fear of their fear and do not be troubled. But hallow the Lord Christ in your hearts. Be ready always with an answer to everyone who asks a reason for the hope that is in you. Yet do so with gentleness and fear, having a good conscience, so that wherein they speak in disparagement of you they who revile your good behavior in Christ may be put to shame. For it is better, if the will of God should so will, that you suffer for doing good than for doing evil. Because Christ also died once for sins, the Just for the unjust, that he might bring us to God. Put to death indeed in the flesh, he was brought to life in the spirit, in which also he went and preached to those spirits that were in prison. These in times past had been disobedient when the patience of God waited in the days of Noe while the ark was building. In that ark a few, that is, eight souls were saved through water. Its counterpart, Baptism, now saves you also (not the putting off of the filth of the flesh, but the inquiry of a good conscience after God), through the resurrection of Jesus Christ; who is at the right hand of God, swallowing up death that we might be made heirs of eternal life; for he went into heaven, Angels, Powers and Virtues being made subject to him.

Since Christ therefore has suffering in the flesh, do you also arm yourselves with the same intent; because he who has suffered in the flesh has ceased from sins; that during the rest of his time in the flesh he may live no longer according to the lusts of men, but according to the will of God. For sufficient is the time past for those to have accomplished the desire of the pagans, walking, as they did, in dissipation, lusts, drunkenness, revellings, carousings and unlawful worship of idols. They are amazed that you do not run with them into the same flood of dissipation, and they abuse you. But they will render an account to him who is ready to judge the living and the dead. For to this end was the gospel preached even to the dead, that they may be judged indeed as men in flesh but may live as God lives in spirit.

III. CHRISTIAN SERVICE AND THE COMING JUDGMENT

But the end of all things is at hand. Be prudent therefore and watchful in prayers. But above all things have a constant mutual charity among yourselves; for charity covers a multitude of sins. Be hospitable to one another without murmuring. According to the gift that each has received, administer it to one another as good stewards of the manifold grace of God. If anyone speaks, let it be with words of God. If anyone ministers, let it be as from the strength that God furnishes; that in all things God may be honored through Jesus Christ, to whom are the glory and the dominion forever. Amen.

Beloved, do not be startled at the trial by fire that is taking place among you to prove you, as if something strange were happening to you; but rejoice, in so far as you are partakers of the sufferings of Christ, that you may also rejoice with exultation in the revelation of his glory. If you are up-braided for the name of Christ, blessed will you be, because the honor, the glory and the power of God and his Spirit rest upon you. Let none of you suffer as a murderer, or a thief, or a slanderer, or as one coveting what belongs to others. But if he suffer as a Christian, let him not be ashamed, but let him glorify God under this name. For the time has come for the judgment to begin with the household of God; but if it begins first with us, what will be the end of those who do not believe the gospel of God? And if the just man scarcely will be saved, where will the impious and the sinner appear? Therefore let them also who suffer according to the will of God commend their souls in well-doing to a faithful Creator.

Now I exhort the presbyters among you—I, your fellow-presbyter and witness of the sufferings of Christ, the partaker also of the glory that is to be revealed in time to come—tend the flock of God which is among you, govern-ing not under constraint, but willingly, according to God; nor yet for the sake of base gain, but eagerly; nor yet as lording it over your charges, but becoming from the heart a pattern to the flock. And when the Prince of the shepherds appears, you will receive the unfading crown of glory.

Likewise, you who are younger, be subject to the presby-ters. And all of you practise humility towards one another; for, "God resists the proud, but gives grace to the humble." Humble yourselves, therefore, under the mighty hand of God, that he may exalt you in the time of visitation; cast all your anxiety upon him, because he cares for you. Be sober, be watchful! For your adversary the devil, as a roaring lion, goes about seeking someone to devour. Resist him, steadfast in the faith, knowing that the same suffering befalls your brethren all over the world. But the God of all grace, who has called us unto his eternal glory in Christ Jesus, will himself, after we have suffered a little while, perfect, strengthen and establish us. To him is the dominion forever and ever. Amen.

CONCLUSION

By Silvanus, the faithful brother as I account him, I have written to you thus briefly, exhorting and testifying that this is the true grace of God. Stand firm in it. The church which is at Babylon, chosen together with you, greets you; and so does my son Mark. Greet one another with a holy kiss. Grace be to you all who are in Christ. Amen.

A Note about
The Second Epistle of St. Peter the Apostle

In this Second Epistle St. Peter refers to his previous letter and to the doctrine contained in it. It was most likely addressed to the same Christian communities of Asia Minor as the former Epistle, and was occasioned by the appearance among the Christians of false teachers, heretics, and deceivers, who promised them freedom, corrupting their good morals and denying the Second Coming of Christ and the end of the world. Its purpose, therefore, was to encourage the Christians to persevere in the faith and to protect them against the dangers of false teachers.

The contents of this Epistle, especially chapter 2, bear such a striking resemblance to the Epistle of St. Jude that it seems probable St. Peter was familiar with the Epistle of his fellow-Apostle and made use of some of its thoughts.

The author calls himself "Simon Peter, a servant and Apostle of Jesus Christ." This statement of authorship is confirmed by the Epistle itself, the author of which describes himself as an eyewitness of our Lord's Transfiguration, and calls Paul his dear brother.

The time and place of its composition are deduced from

1:13–15. The Apostle knows that his death is close at hand. As St. Peter died a martyr in Rome, we may conclude that the Epistle was written from Rome during his imprisonment, A.D. 66–67.

The Second Epistle of St. Peter the Apostle

INTRODUCTION

Simon Peter, a servant and apostle of Jesus Christ, to those who have obtained an equal privilege of faith with ourselves through the justice of our God and Savior Jesus Christ. May grace and peace be given you in abundance in the knowledge of our Lord.

I. CHRISTIAN VIRTUE—
ITS NECESSITY AND MOTIVES

For indeed his divine power has granted us all things pertaining to life and piety through the knowledge of him who has called us by his own glory and power—through which he has granted us the very great and precious promises, so that through them you may become partakers of the divine nature, having escaped from the corruption of that lust which is in the world. Do you accordingly on your part strive diligently to supply your faith with virtue, your virtue with knowledge, your knowledge with self-control, your self-control with patience, your patience with piety, your piety with fraternal love, your fraternal love with charity.

For if you possess these virtues and they abound in you, they will render you neither inactive nor unfruitful in the knowledge of our Lord Jesus Christ. For he who lacks them is blind, groping his way, and has forgotten that he has been cleansed from his former sins. Therefore, brethren, strive even more by good works to make your calling and election sure. For if you do this, you will not fall into sin at any time. Indeed, in this way will be amply provided for you the entrance into the everlasting kingdom of our Lord and Savior Jesus Christ.

Therefore I shall begin to remind you always of these things; although indeed you know them and are well established in the present truth. As long as I am in this tabernacle, I think it right to arouse you by a reminder, knowing as I do that the putting off of my tabernacle is at hand, just as our Lord Jesus Christ signified to me. Moreover I will endeavor that even after my death you may often have occasion to call these things to mind.

For we were not following fictitious tales when we made known to you the power and coming of our Lord Jesus Christ, but we had been eyewitnesses of his grandeur. For he received from God the Father honor and glory, when from out the majestic glory a voice came down to him, speaking thus: "This is my beloved Son in whom I am well pleased." And this voice we ourselves heard borne from heaven when we were with him on the holy mount.

And we have the word of prophecy, surer still, to which you do well to attend, as to a lamp shining in a dark place, until the day dawns and the morning star rises in your hearts. This, then, you must understand first of all, that no prophecy of Scripture is made by private interpretation. For not by will of man was prophecy brought at any time; but holy men of God spoke as they were moved by the Holy Spirit.

II. FALSE TEACHERS

But there were false prophets also among the people, just as among you there will be lying teachers who will bring in destructive sects. They even disown the Lord who bought them, thus bringing upon themselves swift destruction. And many will follow their wanton conduct, and because of them the way of truth will be maligned. And out of greed they will with deceitful words use you for their gain. Their condemnation, passed of old, is not made void, and their destruction does not slumber.

For God did not spare the angels when they sinned, but dragged them down by infernal ropes to Tartarus, and delivered them to be tortured and kept in custody for judgment. Nor did he spare the ancient world, but preserved (with seven others) Noe a herald of justice, when he brought a flood upon the world of the impious. And he condemned the cities of Sodom and Gomorrah to destruction, reducing them to ashes, thus making them an example to those who in the future should live impiously; whereas he delivered just Lot, who was distressed by the lawless behavior of the wicked. For by what that just man saw and heard while dwelling among them, they tormented his just soul day after day with their wicked deeds. The Lord knows how to deliver the God-fearing from temptation and to reserve the wicked for torment on the day of judgment, but especially those who follow the flesh in unclean lust and despise authority.

Rash and self-willed, such men in their deriding do not regard majesty; whereas angels, though greater in strength and power, do not bring against themselves an abusive charge. But these men, like irrational animals created by nature for capture and destruction, deride what they do not understand, and will perish in their own corruption, receiving thereby the recompense of their wrongdoing. They regard as pleasure their daylight revelry; they are spots and blemishes, they abound in wantonness while banqueting with you. They have eyes full of adultery and turned unceasingly towards sin. They entice unstable souls; they have their hearts exercised in covetousness; they are children of a curse. They have forsaken the right way and have gone astray; they have followed the way of Balaam, the son of Bosor, who loved the wages of wrongdoing. But he was rebuked for his madness; a dumb beast of burden spoke with the voice of a man and checked the folly of the prophet.

These men are springs without water and mists driven by storms; the blackness of darkness is reserved for them. For by high-sounding, empty words they entice with sensual allurements of carnal passion those who are just escaping from such as live in error. They promise them freedom, whereas they themselves are the slaves of corruption; for by whatever a man is overcome, of this also he is the slave. For if after escaping the defilements of the world through the knowledge of our Lord and Savior Jesus Christ, they are again entangled therein and overcome, their latter state has become worse for them than the former. For it was better for them not to have known the way of justice, than having known it, to turn back from the holy commandment delivered to them. For what the true proverb says has happened to them, "A dog returns to his vomit," and, "A sow even after washing wallows in the mire."

This, beloved, is now the second epistle that I am writing to you wherein I stir up your pure mind to remembrance, that you may be mindful of what I formerly preached of the words of the holy prophets and of your apostles, which are the precepts of the Lord and Savior. This first you must know, that in the last days there will come deceitful scoffers, men walking according to their own lusts, saying, "Where is the promise or his coming? For since the fathers fell asleep, all things continue as they were from the beginning of creation." For of this they are willfully ignorant, that there were heavens long ago, and an earth formed out of water and by water through the word of God. By these means the world that then was, deluged with water, perished. But the heavens that now are, and the earth, by that same word have been stored up, being reserved for fire against the day of judgment and destruction of ungodly men.

But, beloved, do not be ignorant of this one thing, that one day with the Lord is as a thousand years, and a thousand years as one day. The Lord does not delay in his promises, but for your sake is long-suffering, not wishing that any should perish but that all should turn to repentance. But the day of the Lord will come as a thief; at that time the heavens will pass away with great violence, and the elements will be dissolved with heat, and the earth, and the works that are in it, will be burned up. Seeing therefore that all these things are to be dissolved, what manner of men ought you to be in holy and pious behavior, you who await and hasten towards the coming of the day of God, by which the heavens, being on fire, will be dissolved and the elements will melt away by reason of the heat of the fire! But we look for new heavens and a new earth, according to his promises, wherein dwells justice.

CONCLUSION

Therefore, beloved, while you look for these things, endeavor to be found by him without spot and blameless, in peace. And regard the long-suffering of our Lord as salvation. Just as our most dear brother Paul also, according to the wisdom given him, has written to you, as indeed he did in all his epistles, speaking in them of these things. In these epistles there are certain things difficult to understand, which the unlearned and the unstable distort, just as they do the rest of the Scriptures also, to their own destruction.

You therefore, brethren, since you know this beforehand, be on your guard lest, carried away by the error of the foolish, you fall away from your own steadfastness. But grow in peace and knowledge of our Lord and Savior, Jesus Christ. To him be the glory, both now and to the day of eternity. Amen.

A Note *about*
The First Epistle of St. John the Apostle

St. John the Apostle, the author of the Fourth Gospel, is also the author of this Epistle. Many commentators are of the opinion that the Epistle was written shortly before or shortly after the Gospel to serve as an introduction or a postscript, to it, or at least with the intention that both should be read together. Beyond this, there is nothing to indicate the time and place of its composition; but from this close connection we may say that it was written at Ephesus towards the close of the first century.

The Apostle wrote this letter probably as a pastoral or circular letter to the faithful of Asia Minor, to remind them of what he had written and preached concerning the divinity of Christ—and thus to strengthen them against the heresies of the day. For it seems certain that, in the churches to which the letter is directed, there had risen false teachers and prophets—antichrists who denied that Jesus was the Messias, and Incarnate Son of God.

The fundamental thought of the Epistle is this: God is made known to us in Jesus Christ; hence, fellowship with the Father is through the Son. There are three main currents of thought: (1) God is light; (2) God is justice; (3) God is love.

Hence, if we are to have fellowship with the Father through the Son, we must walk in light, in justice or holiness, and in love. Thus the Apostle calls those who deny that Jesus Christ is the Christ and the Incarnate Son of God, liars and antichrists. He especially emphasizes the sublimity and excellence of love, the love of God finding expression in brotherly love. The Apostle further shows how to distinguish the children of God from the children of the devil; he describes the baseness and gravity of sin; and finally, he shows how the sinner may hope for pardon.

The First Epistle of St. John the Apostle

INTRODUCTION

I write of what was from the beginning, what we have heard, what we have seen with our eyes, what we have looked upon and our hands have handled: of the Word of Life. And the Life was made known and we have seen, and now testify and announce to you, the Life Eternal which was with the Father, and has appeared to us. What we have seen and have heard we announce to you, in order that you also may have fellowship with us, and that our fellowship may be with the Father, and with his Son Jesus Christ. And these things we write to you that you may rejoice, and our joy may be full.

I. GOD IS LIGHT

And the message which we have heard from him and announce to you, is this: that God is light, and in him is no darkness. If we say that we have fellowship with him, and walk in darkness, we lie, and are not practising the truth.

But if we walk in the light as he also is in the light, we have fellowship with one another, and the blood of Jesus Christ, his Son, cleanses us from all sin.

If we say that we have no sin, we deceive ourselves, and the truth is not in us. If we acknowledge our sins, he is faithful and just to forgive us our sins and to cleanse us from all iniquity. If we say that we have not sinned, we make him a liar, and his word is not in us.

My dear children, these things I write to you in order that you may not sin. But if anyone sins, we have an advocate with the Father, Jesus Christ, the just; and he is a propitiation for our sins, not for ours only but also for those of the whole world.

And by this we can be sure that we know him, if we keep his commandments. He who says that he knows him, and does not keep his commandments, is a liar and the truth is not in him. But he who keeps his word, in him the love of God is truly perfected; and by this we know that we are in him. He who says that he abides in him, ought himself also to walk just as he walked.

Beloved, no new commandment am I writing to you, but an old commandment which you had from the beginning. The old commandment is the word which you have heard. Again, a new commandment I am writing to you, and this is true both in him and in you. Because the darkness has passed away and the true light is now shining. He who says that he is in the light, and hates his brother, is in the darkness still. He who loves his brother abides in the light, and for him there is no stumbling. But he who hates his brother is in the darkness, and walks in the darkness, and he does not know whither he goes; because the darkness has blinded his eyes.

I am writing to you, dear children, because your sins are forgiven you for his name's sake. I am writing to you, fathers, because you know him who is from the beginning. I am writing to you, young men, because you have conquered the evil one. I am writing to you, little ones, because you know the Father. I am writing to you, fathers, because you know him who is from the beginning. I am writing to you, young men, because you are strong and the word of God abides in you, and you have conquered the evil one. Do not love the world, or the things that are in the world. If anyone loves the world, the love of the Father is not in him; because all that is in the world is the lust of the flesh, and the lust of the eyes, and the pride of life; which is not from the Father, but from the world. And the world with its lust is passing away, but he who does the will of God abides forever.

Dear children, it is the last hour; and as you have heard that Antichrist is coming, so now many antichrists have arisen; whence we know that it is the last hour. They have gone forth from us, but they were not of us. For if they had been of us, they would surely have continued with us; but they were to be made manifest, that not one of them is of us. But you have an anointing from the Holy One and you know all things. I have not written to you as to those who do not know the truth, but as to those who know it, and because no lie is of the truth. Who is the liar but he who denies that Jesus is the Christ? He is the Antichrist who denies the Father and the Son. No one who disowns the Son has the Father. He who confesses the Son has the Father also. As for you, let that which you have heard from the beginning abide in you. If that abides in you which you have heard from the beginning, you also will abide in the Son and in the Father. And this is the promise that he has given us, the life everlasting.

These things I have written to you concerning those who lead you astray. And as for you, let the anointing which you have received from him, dwell in you, and you have no need that anyone teach you. But as his anointing teaches you concerning all things, and is true and is no lie, even as it has taught you, abide in him.

II. GOD IS JUSTICE

And now, dear children, abide in him, so that when he appears we may have confidence, and may not shrink ashamed from him at his coming. If you know that he is just, know that everyone also who does what is just has been born of him.

Behold what manner of love the Father has bestowed upon us, that we should be called children of God; and such we are. This is why the world does not know us, because it did not know him. Beloved, now we are the children of God, and it has not yet appeared what we shall be. We know that, when he appears, we shall be like to him, for we shall see him just as he is. And everyone who has this hope in him makes himself holy, just as he also is holy.

Everyone who commits sin commits iniquity also; and sin is iniquity. And you know that he appeared to take our sins away, and sin is not in him. No one who abides in him commits sin; and no one who sins has seen him, or has known him.

Dear children, let no one lead you astray. He who does

what is just is just, even as he is just. He who commits sin is of the devil, because the devil sins from the beginning. To this end the Son of God appeared, that he might destroy the works of the devil. Whoever is born of God does not commit sin, because his seed abides in him and he cannot sin, because he is born of God. In this the children of God and the children of the devil are made known.

Whoever is not just is not of God, nor is he just who does not love his brother. For this is the message that you have heard from the beginning, that we should love one another; not like Cain, who was of the evil one, and killed his brother. And wherefore did he kill him? Because his own works were wicked, but his brother's just. Do not be surprised, brethren, if the world hates you. We know that we have passed from death to life, because we love the brethren. He who does not love abides in death. Everyone who hates his brother is a murderer. And you know that no murderer has eternal life abiding in him.

In this we come to know his love, that he laid down his life for us; and we likewise ought to lay down our life for the brethren. He who has the goods of this world and sees his brother in need and closes his heart to him, how does the love of God abide in him? My dear children, let us not love in word, neither with the tongue, but in deed and in truth.

In this we know that we are of the truth, and in his sight we set our hearts at rest. Because if our heart blames us, God is greater than our heart and knows all things. Beloved, if our heart does not condemn us, we have confidence towards God; and whatever we ask, we shall receive from him, because we keep his commandments and do those things that are pleasing in his sight.

And this is his commandment, that we should believe in the name of his Son Jesus Christ, and love one another, even as he gave us commandment. And he who keeps his commandments abides in God, and God in him. And in this we know that he abides in us, by the Spirit whom he has given us.

Beloved, do not believe every spirit, but test the spirits to see whether they are of God; because many false prophets have gone forth into the world. By this is the spirit of God known: every spirit that confesses that Jesus Christ has come in the flesh, is of God. And every spirit that severs Jesus, is not of God, but is of Antichrist, of whom you have heard that he is coming, and now is already in the world.

You are of God, dear children, and have overcome him, because greater is he who is in you than he who is in the world. They are of the world; therefore of the world they speak and the world listens to them. We are of God. He who knows God listens to us; he who is not of God does not listen to us. By this we know the spirit of truth and the spirit of error.

III. GOD IS LOVE

Beloved, let us love one another, for love is from God. And everyone who loves is born of God, and knows God. He who does not love does not know God; for God is love. In this has the love of God been shown in our case, that God has sent his only-begotten Son into the world that we may live through him. In this is the love, not that we have loved God, but that he has first loved us, and sent his Son a propitiation for our sins. Beloved, if God has so loved us, we also ought to love one another.

No one has ever seen God. If we love one another, God abides in us and his love is perfected in us. In this we know that we abide in him and he in us, because he has given us of his Spirit. And we have seen, and do testify, that the Father has sent his Son to be Savior of the world. Whoever confesses that Jesus is the Son of God, God abides in him and he in God. And we have come to know, and have believed, the love that God has in our behalf. God is love, and he who abides in love abides in God, and God in him.

In this is love perfected with us, that we may have confidence in the day of judgment; because as he is, even so are we also in this world. There is no fear in love; but perfect love casts out fear, because fear brings punishment. And he who fears is not perfected in love. Let us therefore love, because God first loved us. If anyone says, "I love God," and hates his brother, he is a liar. For how can he who does not love his brother, whom he sees, love God, whom he does not see? And this commandment we have from him, that he who loves God should love his brother also.

Everyone who believes that Jesus is the Christ is born of God. And everyone who loves him who begot, loves also the one begotten of him. In this we know that we love the children of God, when we love God and do his commandments. For this is the love of God, that we keep his commandments; and his commandments are not burdensome. Because all that is born of God overcomes the world; and this is the victory that overcomes the world, our faith. Who is there that overcomes the world if not he who believes that Jesus is the Son of God?

This is he who came in water and in blood, Jesus Christ; not in the water only, but in the water and in the blood. And it is the Spirit that bears witness that Christ is the truth. For there are three that bear witness [in heaven: the Father, the Word, and the Holy Spirit; and these three are one. And there are three that bear witness on earth]: the Spirit, and the water, and the blood; and these three are one. If we receive the testimony of men, the testimony of God is greater; for this is the testimony of God which is greater, that he has borne witness concerning his Son. He who believes in the Son of God has the testimony of God in himself. He who does not believe the Son, makes him a liar; because he does not believe the witness that God has borne concerning his son.

And this is the testimony, that God has given us eternal life; and this life is in his Son. He who has the Son has the life. He who has not the Son has not the life.

These things I am writing to you that you may know that you have eternal life—you who believe in the name of the Son of God.

And the confidence that we have towards him is this, that if we ask anything according to his will, he hears us. And we know that he hears us whatever we ask; we know that the requests we make of him are granted.

He who knows his brother is committing a sin that is not unto death, shall ask, and shall give life to him who does not commit a sin unto death. There is sin unto death; I do not mean that anyone should ask as to that. All lawlessness is sin, and there is a sin unto death.

CONCLUSION

We know that no one who is born of God commits sin; but the Begotten of God preserves him and the evil one does not touch him. We know that we are of God, and the whole world is in the power of the evil one. And we know that the Son of God has come and has given us understanding, that we may know the true God and may be in his true Son. He is the true God and eternal life.

Dear children, guard yourselves from the idols. Amen.

A Note *about*
The Second Epistle of St. John the Apostle

The ideas and expressions of the Second Epistle are the same as those of the First; hence its composition must have been prompted by the same or similar occasions. It was probably written towards the end of the first century.

The recipient of the Second Epistle is addressed as "Elect Lady." The meaning of the title is obscure. Many have thought that an individual refers to one whose name was Kuria or Elect, or simply "an elect lady." Others have seen in the title a mere symbol, either of the universal Church or of some particular church in Asia Minor.

The Apostle commends the recipients of the letter for their steadfastness in the true faith and exhorts them to persevere, lest they lose the reward of their labors. He exhorts them to love one another, but warns them to have no fellowship with heretics—and not even to greet them.

The Second Epistle of St. John the Apostle

INTRODUCTION

The Presbyter to the Elect Lady and to her children whom I love in truth—and not I alone, but also all who have known the truth—for the sake of the truth which abides in us, and will be with us forever: grace, mercy and peace be with you from God the Father and from Christ Jesus, the Son of the Father, in truth and love.

TEACHING OF THE APOSTLE

I rejoiced greatly that I found some of thy children walking in truth, according to the commandment that we have received from the Father. And now I beseech thee, lady, not as writing to thee a new commandment, but that which we have had from the beginning, that we love one another. And this is love, that we walk according to his commandments. This is the commandment, that, just as you have heard from the beginning, you should walk in it.

For many deceivers have gone forth into the world who do not confess Jesus as the Christ coming in the flesh. This is the deceiver and the Antichrist.

Look to yourselves, that you do not lose what you have worked for, but that you may receive a full reward. Anyone who advances and does not abide in the doctrine of Christ, has not God; he who abides in the doctrine, he has both the Father and the Son. If anyone come to you and does not bring this doctrine, do not receive him into the house, or say to him, "Welcome." For he who says to him, "Welcome," is sharer in his evil works.

CONCLUSION

Though I have much to write to you, I do not wish to do so with paper and ink; for I hope to be with you and to speak face to face, that your joy may be full.

The children of thy sister Elect greet you.

A Note *about*
The Third Epistle of St. John the Apostle

The Third Epistle of St. John is addressed to a certain Gaius. Whether he is to be identified with a Christian of the same name mentioned in Acts 19:29 and 20:4 is uncertain.

The time and place of composition of this Epistle are likewise uncertain. The similarity of content and form, however, suggests that it was written about the same time as the Second Epistle.

The Epistle, though brief, vividly portrays certain features in the life of the early Church. Gaius is praised for his hospitality and for walking in the truth. Diotrephes, on the contrary, is censured for his ambition and lack of hospitality. A certain Demetrius is also commended for his virtue.

The Third Epistle of St. John the Apostle

INTRODUCTION

The Presbyter to the beloved Gaius, whom I love in truth.

PRAISE OF GAIUS

Beloved, I pray that in all things thou mayest prosper and be in health, even as thy soul prospers. I rejoiced greatly when some brethren came and bore witness to thy truth, even as thou walkest in the truth. I have no greater joy than to hear that my children are walking in the truth. Beloved, thou dost in accordance with faith whatever thou workest for the brethren, and that even when they are strangers. They have borne witness to thy love before the church. Thou wilt do well to see them off on their journey in a manner worthy of God. For on behalf of the Name they have gone forth, taking nothing from the pagans. We therefore ought to support such as these, that we may be fellow-workers for the truth.

DIOTREPHES AND DEMETRIUS

I would have written perhaps to the church; but Diotrephes, who loves to have the first place among them, does not receive us. Therefore if I come, I will recall to mind his works, prating against us with evil words; and as if this were not enough for him, he himself does not receive the brethren, and those who do so he hinders, and casts them out of the church.

Beloved, do not imitate evil, but that which is good. He who does what is good is of God; he who does what is evil has not seen God. Witness is borne to Demetrius by all, and by the truth itself, yes, we also bear witness; and thou knowest that our witness is true.

CONCLUSION

I had much to write to thee; but I do not want to write to thee with pen and ink. But I hope to see thee shortly, and we will speak face to face.

Peace be to thee. The friends greet thee. Greet the friends by name.

A *Note about*
The Epistle of St. Jude the Apostle

The Epistle is both brief and practical. It was occasioned by the teachings and practices of certain heretics within the Church. By their evil lives they were denying that Jesus is the only Lord and Master. They were opposed to all law and authority, and they changed Christian liberty into un-restrained license. The Epistle is a warning to them.

The Epistle of St. Jude the Apostle

INTRODUCTION

Jude, the servant of Jesus Christ and the brother of James,
to the called who have been loved in God the Father and
preserved for Christ Jesus: mercy and peace and charity be
given you in abundance.

Beloved, while I was making every endeavor to write to
you about our common salvation, I found it necessary to
write to you, exhorting you to contend earnestly for the
faith once for all delivered to the saints. For certain men
have stealthily entered in, who long ago were marked out
for this condemnation, ungodly men who turn the grace
of God into wantonness and disown our only Master and
Lord, Jesus Christ.

I. WARNING AGAINST FALSE TEACHERS

But I desire to remind you, though once for all you have
come to know all things, that Jesus, who saved the people

from the land of Egypt, the next time destroyed those who did not believe. And the angels also who did not preserve their original state, but forsook their abode, he has kept in everlasting chains under darkness for the judgment of the great day. Just as Sodom and Gomorrah, and the neighboring cities which like them committed sins of immorality and practised unnatural vice, have been made an example, undergoing the punishment of eternal fire.

In like manner do these men also defile the flesh, disregard authority, deride majesty. Yet when Michael the archangel was fiercely disputing with the devil about the body of Moses, he did not venture to bring against him an accusation of blasphemy, but said, "May the Lord rebuke thee." But these men deride whatever they do not know; and the things they know by instinct like the dumb beasts, become for them a source of destruction. Woe to them! for they have gone in the way of Cain, and have rushed on thoughtlessly into the error of Balaam for the sake of gain, and have perished in the rebellion of Core. These men are stains on their feasts, banqueting together without fear, looking after themselves; clouds without water, carried about by the winds; trees in the fall, unfruitful, twice dead, uprooted; wild waves of the sea, foaming up their shame; wandering stars, for whom the storm of darkness has been reserved forever.

Now of these also Henoch, the seventh from Adam, prophesied, saying, "Behold, the Lord has come with thousands of his holy ones to execute judgment upon all, and to convict all the impious of all their impious works, and of all the hard things that impious sinners have spoken against him." These are grumbling murmurers walking according to their lusts. And haughty in speech, they cultivate people for the sake of gain. But as for you, beloved, be mindful of the words that have been spoken beforehand by the apostles of our Lord Jesus Christ, who kept saying to you that at the end of time there will come scoffers, walking impiously according to their lusts. These are they who set themselves apart, sensual men, not having the Spirit.

II. ADMONITIONS FOR CHRISTIANS

But as for you, beloved, build up yourselves upon your most holy faith, praying in the Holy Spirit. Keep yourselves in the love of God, looking for the mercy of our Lord Jesus Christ unto life everlasting. And some, who are judged, reprove; but others, save, snatching them from the fire. And to others be merciful with fear, hating even the garment which is soiled by the flesh.

CONCLUSION

Now to him who is able to preserve you without sin and to set you before the presence of his glory, without blemish, in gladness, to the only God our Savior, through Jesus Christ our Lord, belong glory and majesty, dominion and authority, before all time, and now, and forever. Amen.

A Note about
The Revelation of St. John the Apostle

The book of Revelation is a revelation of the things that were, are, and will be. We are actually witnessing some of the events foretold in this book, but many still lie in the future. It is Christ who commands John to write to the seven churches, opens the seven seals, reveals the sufferings of the saints, opens the little book, overcomes the beast, reigns during the period of the first resurrection, judges the dead, both great and small, according to their works at His Second Coming, rules over all things from the beginning, presides over all the changing scenes of earth's history, and is the King of kings and Lord of lords.

The book is one of hope, but also one of warning; its aim is to assure the Church of the advent of her Lord in victory. The precise time of this victory lies hidden with God, but it is certain, although the crown will not be won without a struggle. Heaven will be stormed and carried away through suffering and conflict. And all who keep the words of this book will take part in the conflict and share in the victory.

The conflict is presented under the form of symbols. It is not easy to give a full interpretation of all the types, but the general symbols are not difficult to understand. Jerusalem stands as the type of the good cause, and this is the Church of Christ. Babylon appears as the type of the evil cause, and this is the world power. The heavenly Jerusalem has the assistance of divine power. The earthly Babylon has the help of evil powers, the dragon, the beast and the false prophet. The scenes in the great conflict arrange themselves around these types of good and of evil. The numbers, the seals, the trumpets, and the bowls are phases in the development and consummation of the conflict.

John has arranged the scenes in a sevenfold structure; even in the subordinate visions he keeps to this arrangement. Commentators, however, are not agreed in marking off the limits of each structure.

The book was written in Greek by St. John the Evangelist, on the island of Patmos, about the year A.D. 96.

The Revelation of St. John the Apostle

PROLOGUE

The revelation of Jesus Christ which God gave him, to make known to his servants the things that must shortly come to pass; and he sent and signified them through his angel to his servant John; who bore witness to the word of God and to the testimony of Jesus Christ, to whatever he saw. Blessed is he who reads and those who hear the words of this prophecy, and keep the things that are written therein; for the time is at hand.

John to the seven churches that are in Asia: grace be to you and peace from him who is and who was and who is coming, and from the seven spirits who are before his throne, and from Jesus Christ, who is the faithful witness, the firstborn of the dead, and the ruler of the kings of the earth. To him who has loved us, and washed us from our sins in his own blood, and made us to be a kingdom, and priests to God his Father—to him belong glory and dominion forever and ever. Amen.

Behold, he comes with the clouds, and every eye shall

see him, and they also who pierced him. And all the tribes of the earth shall wail over him. Even so. Amen. "I am the Alpha and the Omega, the beginning and the end," says the Lord God, "who is and who was and who is coming, the Almighty."

I. THE SEVEN LETTERS

I, John, your brother and partner in the tribulation and kingdom and patience that are in Jesus, was on the island which is called Patmos, because of the word of God and the testimony of Jesus. I was in the spirit on the Lord's day, and I heard behind me a great voice, as of a trumpet, saying, "What thou seest write in a book, and send to the seven churches, to Ephesus, and to Smyrna, and to Pergamum, and to Thyatira, and to Sardis, and to Philadelphia, and to Laodicea."

And I turned to see the voice that was speaking to me. And having turned, I saw seven golden lamp-stands; and in the midst of the seven lamp-stands One like a son of man, clothed with a garment reaching to the ankles, and girt about the breasts with a golden girdle. But his head and his hair were white as white wool, and as snow, and his eyes were as a flame of fire; his feet were like fine brass, as in a glowing furnace, and his voice like the voice of many waters. And he had in his right hand seven stars. And out of his mouth came forth a sharp two-edged sword; and his countenance was like the sun shining in its power.

And when I saw him, I fell at his feet as one dead. And he laid his right hand upon me, saying, "Do not be afraid; I am the First and the Last, and he who lives; I was dead, and behold, I am living forevermore; and I have the keys of death and of hell. Write therefore the things that are to come hereafter. As for the mystery of the seven stars that thou sawest in my right hand, and the seven golden lamp-stands—the seven stars are the seven angels of the seven churches, and the seven lamp-stands are the seven churches."

"To the angel of the church at Ephesus write: Thus says he who holds the seven stars in his right hand, who walks in the midst of the seven golden lamp-stands: I know thy works and thy labor and thy patience, and that thou canst not bear evil men; but hast tried them who say they are apostles and are not, and hast found them false. And thou hast patience and hast endured for my name, and hast not grown weary.

"But I have this against thee, that thou hast left thy first love. Remember therefore whence thou hast fallen, and repent and do the former works; or else I will come to thee, and will move thy lamp-stand out of its place, unless thou repentest. But this thou hast: thou hatest the works of the Nicolaites, which I also hate.

"He who has an ear, let him hear what the Spirit says to the churches: He who overcomes I will permit to eat of the tree of life, which is in the paradise of my God.

"And to the angel of the church at Smyrna write: Thus says the First and the Last, who was dead and is alive: I know thy tribulation and thy poverty, but thou art rich; and that thou art slandered by those who say they are Jews and are not, but are a synagogue of Satan. Fear none of those things that thou art about to suffer. Behold, the devil is about to cast some of you into prison that you may be tested, and you will have tribulation for ten days. Be thou faithful unto death, and I will give thee the crown of life.

"He who has an ear, let him hear what the Spirit says to the churches: He who overcomes shall not be hurt by the second death.

"And to the angel of the church at Pergamum write: Thus says he who has the sharp two-edged sword: I know where thou dwellest, where the throne of Satan is: and thou holdest fast my name and didst not disown my faith, even in the days of Antipas, my faithful witness, who was slain among you where Satan dwells.

"But I have a few things against thee, because thou hast there some who hold the teaching of Balaam, who taught Balak to cast a stumbling-block before the children of Israel, that they might eat and commit fornication. So thou hast also some who hold the teaching of the Nicolaites. In like manner repent, or else I will come to thee quickly, and will fight against them with the sword of my mouth.

"He who has an ear, let him hear what the Spirit says to the churches: To him who overcomes, I will give the hidden manna, and I will give him a white pebble, and upon the pebble a new name written, which no one knows except him who receives it.

"And to the angel of the church at Thyatira write: Thus says the Son of God, who has eyes like to a flame of fire, and whose feet are like fine brass: I know thy works, thy faith, thy love, thy ministry, thy patience and thy last works, which are more numerous than the former.

"But I have against thee that thou sufferest the woman Jezebel, who calls herself a prophetess, to teach, and to seduce my servants, to commit fornication, and to eat of things sacrificed to idols. And I gave her time that she might repent, and she does not want to repent of her immorality. Behold, I will cast her upon a bed, and those who commit adultery with her into great tribulation, unless they repent of their deeds. And her children I will strike with death, and all the churches shall know that I am he who searches desires and hearts, and I will give to each of you according to your works.

"But to you I say, to the rest in Thyatira, as many as do not hold this teaching and do not know the depths of Satan, as they call them, I will not put upon you any other burden. But that which you have, hold fast till I come. And to him who overcomes, and who keeps my works unto the end, I will give authority over nations. And he shall rule them with a rod of iron, and like the potter's vessel they shall be dashed to pieces, as I also have received from my Father; and I will give him the morning star.

"He who has an ear, let him hear what the Spirit says to the churches.

"And to the angel of the church at Sardis write: Thus says he who has the seven spirits of God and the seven stars: I know thy works; thou hast the name of being alive, and thou art dead. Be watchful and strengthen the things that remain, but which were ready to die. For I do not find thy works complete before my God. Remember therefore what thou hast received and heard, and observe it and repent. Therefore, if thou wilt not watch, I will come upon thee as a thief, and thou shalt not know at what hour I shall come upon thee. But thou hast a few persons at Sardis who have not defiled their garments, and they shall walk with me in white; for they are worthy. He who overcomes shall be arrayed thus in white garments, and I will not blot his name out of the book of life, but I will confess his name before my Father, and before his angels.

"He who has an ear, let him hear what the Spirit says to the churches.

"And to the angel of the church at Philadelphia write: Thus says the holy one, the true one, he who has the key of David, he who opens and no one shuts, and who shuts and no one opens: I know thy works. Behold, I have caused a door to be opened before thee which no one can shut, for thou hast scanty strength, and thou hast kept my word and hast not disowned my name. Behold, I will bring some of the synagogue of Satan who say they are Jews, and are not, but are lying—behold, I will make them come and worship before thy feet. And they shall know that I have loved thee. Because thou hast kept the word of my patience, I too will keep thee from the hour of trial, which is about to come upon the whole world to try those who dwell upon the earth. I come quickly; hold fast what thou hast, that no one receive thy crown. He who overcomes, I will make him a pillar in the temple of my God, and never more shall he go outside. And I will write upon him the name of my God, and the name of the city of my God—the new Jerusalem, which comes down out of heaven from my God—and my new name.

"He who has an ear, let him hear what the Spirit says to the churches.

"And to the angel of the church at Laodicea write: Thus says the Amen, the faithful and true witness, who is the beginning of the creation of God: I know thy works; thou art neither cold nor hot. I would that thou wert cold or hot. But because thou art lukewarm, and neither cold nor hot,

I am about to vomit thee out of my mouth; because thou sayest, 'I am rich and have grown wealthy and have need of nothing,' and dost not know that thou art the wretched and miserable and poor and blind and naked one.

"I counsel thee to buy of me gold refined by fire, that thou mayest become rich, and mayest be clothed in white garments, and that the shame of thy nakedness may not appear, and to anoint thy eyes with eye salve that thou mayest see. As for me, those whom I love I rebuke and chastise. Be earnest therefore and repent. Behold, I stand at the door and knock. If any man listens to my voice and opens the door to me, I will come in to him and will sup with him, and he with me. He who overcomes, I will permit him to sit with me upon my throne; as I also have overcome and have sat with my Father on his throne.

"He who has an ear, let him hear what the Spirit says to the churches."

II. THE SEVEN SEALS

After this I looked, and behold, a door standing open in heaven, and the former voice, which I had heard as of a trumpet speaking with me, said, "Come up hither, and I will show thee the things that must come to pass hereafter." Immediately I was in the spirit; and behold, there was a throne set in heaven, and upon the throne One was sitting. And he who sat was in appearance like to a jasper-stone and a sardius, and there was a rainbow round about the throne, in appearance like to an emerald.

And round about the throne are twenty-four seats; and

upon the seats twenty-four elders sitting, clothed in white garments, and on their heads crowns of gold. And from the throne proceed flashes of lightning, rumblings, and peals of thunder; and there are seven lamps burning before the throne, which are the seven spirits of God. And before the throne there is, as it were, a sea of glass like to crystal, and in the midst of the throne, and round the throne, are four living creatures, full of eyes before and behind. And the first living creature is like a lion and the second like a calf, and the third has the face, as it were, of a man, and the fourth is like an eagle flying. And the four living creatures have each of them six wings; round about and within they are full of eyes. And they do not rest day and night, saying, "Holy, holy, holy, the Lord God Almighty, who was, and who is, and who is coming."

And when those living creatures give glory and honor and benediction to him who sits on the throne, who lives forever and ever, the twenty-four elders will fall down before him who sits upon the throne, and will worship him who lives forever and ever, and will cast their crowns before the throne, saying, "Worthy art thou, O Lord our God, to receive glory and honor and power; for thou hast created all things, and because of thy will they existed, and were created."

And I saw upon the right hand of him who sits upon the throne a scroll written within and without, sealed with seven seals. And I saw a strong angel proclaiming with a loud voice, "Who is worthy to open the scroll, and to break the seals thereof?" And no one in heaven, or on earth, or under the earth, was able to open the scroll or to look thereon. And I wept much, because no one was found worthy to open the scroll or to look thereon.

And one of the elders said to me, "Do not weep; behold, the lion of the tribe of Juda, the root of David, has overcome to open the scroll and its seven seals." And I saw, and behold, in the midst of the elders, a Lamb standing, as if slain, having seven horns and seven eyes, which are the seven spirits of God sent forth into all the earth. And he came and took the scroll out of the right hand of him who sat upon the throne. And when he had opened the scroll, the four living creatures and the twenty-four elders fell down before the Lamb, having each a harp and golden bowls full of incense, which are the prayers of the saints.

And they sing a new canticle, saying, "Worthy art thou to take the scroll and to open its seals; for thou wast slain, and hast redeemed us for God with thy blood, out of every tribe and tongue and people and nation, and hast made them for our God a kingdom and priests, and they shall reign over the earth."

And I beheld, and I heard a voice of many angels round about the throne, and the living creatures and the elders, and the number of them was thousands of thousands, saying with a loud voice, "Worthy is the Lamb who was slain to receive power and divinity and wisdom and strength and honor and glory and blessing." And every creature that is in heaven and on the earth and under the earth, and such as are on the sea, and all that are in them, I heard them all saying, "To him who sits upon the throne, and to the Lamb, blessing and honor and glory and dominion, forever and ever." And the four living creatures said, "Amen," and the elders fell down and worshipped him who lives forever and ever.

And I saw that the Lamb had opened the first of the seven

seals, and I heard one of the four living creatures saying, as with a voice of thunder, "Come!" And I saw, and behold, a white horse, and he who was sitting on it had a bow, and there was given him a crown, and he went forth as a conqueror to conquer.

And when he opened the second seal, I heard the second living creature saying, "Come!" And there went forth another horse, a red one; and to him who was sitting on it, it was given to take peace from the earth, and that men should kill one another, and there was given him a great sword.

And when he opened the third seal, I heard the third living creature saying, "Come!" And I saw, and behold, a black horse, and he who was sitting on it had a balance in his hand. And I heard as it were a voice in the midst of the four living creatures, saying, "A measure of wheat for a denarius, and three measures of barley for a denarius, and do not harm the wine and the oil."

And when he opened the fourth seal, I heard the voice of the fourth living creature saying, "Come!" And I saw, and behold, a pale-green horse, and he who was sitting on it—his name is Death, and hell was following him. And there was given him power over the four parts of the earth, to kill with sword, with famine, and with death, and with the beasts of the earth.

And when he opened the fifth seal, I saw under the altar the souls of those who had been slain for the word of God, and for the witness that they bore. And they cried with a loud voice, saying, "How long, O Lord (holy and true), dost thou refrain from judging and from avenging our blood on those who dwell on the earth?" And there was given to each of them a white robe; and they were told to rest a little while longer, until the number of their fellow-servants and their brethren who are to be slain, even as they had been, should be complete.

And I saw, when he opened the sixth seal, and there was a great earthquake, and the sun became black as sackcloth of hair; and the whole moon became as blood. And the stars of heaven fell upon the earth, as the fig tree sheds its unripe figs when it is shaken by a great wind. And heaven passed away as a scroll that is rolled up; and every mountain and the islands were moved out of their places. And the kings of the earth, and the princes, and the tribunes, and the rich, and the strong, and everyone, bond and free, hid themselves in the caves and in the rocks of the mountains. And they said to the mountains and to the rocks, "Fall upon us, and hide us from the face of him who sits upon the throne, and from the wrath of the Lamb; for the great day of their wrath has come, and who is able to stand?"

After this I saw four angels standing at the four corners of the earth, holding fast the four winds of the earth, that no wind should blow over the earth, or over the sea, or upon any tree. And I saw another angel ascending from the rising of the sun, having the seal of the living God; and he cried with a loud voice to the four angels, who had it in their power to harm the earth and the sea, saying, "Do not harm the earth or the sea or the trees, till we have sealed the servants of our God on their foreheads." And I heard the number of those who were sealed, a hundred and forty-four thousand sealed, out of every tribe of the children of Israel; of the tribe of Juda, twelve thousand sealed; of the tribe of Ruben, twelve thousand; of the tribe of Gad, twelve thousand; of the tribe of Aser, twelve thousand; of the tribe of Nephthali, twelve thousand; of the tribe of Manasses, twelve thousand; of the tribe of Simeon, twelve thousand; of the tribe of Levi, twelve thousand; of the tribe of Issachar, twelve thousand; of the tribe of Zabulon, twelve thousand; of the tribe of Joseph, twelve thousand; of the tribe of Benjamin, twelve thousand sealed.

After this I saw a great multitude which no man could number, out of all nations and tribes and peoples and tongues, standing before the throne and before the Lamb, clothed in white robes, and with palms in their hands. And they cried with a loud voice, saying, "Salvation belongs to our God who sits upon the throne, and to the Lamb." And all the angels were standing round about the throne, and the elders and the four living creatures; and they fell on their faces before the throne and worshipped God, saying, "Amen. Blessing and glory and wisdom and thanksgiving and honor and power and strength to our God forever and ever. Amen."

And one of the elders spoke and said to me, "These who are clothed in white robes, who are they? and whence have they come?" And I said to him, "My lord, thou knowest." And he said to me, "These are they who have come out of the great tribulation, and have washed their robes and made them white in the blood of the Lamb. Therefore they are before the throne of God, and serve him day and night in his temple, and he who sits upon the throne will dwell with them. They shall neither hunger nor thirst any more, neither shall the sun strike them nor any heat. For the Lamb who is in the midst of the throne will shepherd them, and will guide them to the fountains of the waters of life, and God will wipe away every tear from their eyes."

And when he opened the seventh seal, there was silence in heaven, as it were for half an hour.

III. THE SEVEN TRUMPETS

And I saw the seven angels who stand before God, and there were given to them seven trumpets. And another angel came and stood before the altar, having a golden censer; and there was given to him much incense, that he might offer it with the prayers of all the saints upon the golden altar which is before the throne. And with the prayers of the saints there went up before God from the angel's hand the smoke of the incense. And the angel took the censer and filled it with the fire of the altar and threw it down upon the earth, and there were peals of thunder, rumblings, and flashes of lightning and an earthquake. And the seven angels who had the seven trumpets prepared themselves to sound the trumpet.

And the first angel sounded the trumpet, and there followed hail and fire mingled with blood, and it was cast upon the earth; and the third part of the earth was burnt up, and the third part of the trees were burnt up, and all green grass was burnt up.

And the second angel sounded the trumpet, and as it were a great mountain burning with fire was cast into the sea; and the third part of the sea became blood, and there died the third part of those creatures that have life in the sea, and the third part of the ships was destroyed.

And the third angel sounded the trumpet, and there fell from heaven a great star, burning like a torch, and it fell upon the third part of the rivers and upon the fountains of water. The name of the star is called Wormwood. And the third part of the waters became wormwood; and many people died of the waters because they were made bitter.

And the fourth angel sounded the trumpet, and the third part of the sun was smitten, and the third part of the moon, and the third part of the stars, that the third part of them might be darkened, and the day for the third part of it might not shine, and the night likewise.

And I beheld, and I heard the voice of an eagle flying in midheaven, saying with a loud voice, "Woe, woe, woe to the inhabitants of the earth!" because of the rest of the trumpet-voices of the three angels who were about to sound the trumpet.

And the fifth angel sounded the trumpet, and I saw that a star had fallen from heaven upon the earth, and there was given to him the key of the bottomless pit. And he opened the bottomless pit, and there came up smoke out of the pit like the smoke of a great furnace; and the sun and the air were darkened by the smoke of the pit. And out of the smoke there came forth locusts upon the earth. And there was given to them power, as the scorpions of the earth have power. And they were told not to hurt the grass of the earth or any green thing or any tree; but only the men who do not have God's seal upon their foreheads. And they were not permitted to kill anyone, but to torture them for five months; and their torment was as the torment of a scorpion when it strikes a man.

And in those days men will seek death and will not find it; and they will long to die and death will flee from them. And in appearance the locusts were like horses made ready for battle; and there were on their heads crowns as it were like gold; and their faces were like the faces of men. And they had hair like the hair of women; and their teeth were like the teeth of lions. And they had breastplates like breastplates of iron; and the sound of their wings was like the sound of many horse-chariots running to battle. And they had tails like those of scorpions and there were stings in their tails; and they had power to harm mankind for five months. And they had over them a king, the angel of the abyss; his name in Hebrew is Abaddon, and in the Greek Apollyon; in Latin he has the name Exterminans.

The first woe is past; behold, two woes are yet to come hereafter!

And the sixth angel sounded the trumpet, and I heard a voice from the four horns of the golden altar which is before God, saying to the sixth angel who had the trumpet, "Loose the four angels who are bound at the great river Euphrates." And the four angels were loosed who had been kept ready for the hour and day and month and year, that they might kill the third part of mankind. And the number of the army of horsemen was twenty thousand times ten thousand. I heard the number of them.

And this is how I saw the horses in the vision: they who sat upon them had breastplates like to fire and to hyacinth and to sulphur, and the heads of the horses were like the heads of lions; and from their mouths issued fire and smoke and sulphur. By these three plagues the third part of mankind was killed, by the fire and the smoke and the sulphur which issued from their mouth. For the power of the horses is in their mouths and in their tails. For their tails are like serpents, and have heads, and with them they do harm.

And the rest of mankind, they who were not killed by

these plagues, did not repent of the works of their hands so as not to worship the demons and the idols of gold and of silver and of brass and of stone and of wood, which can neither see nor hear nor walk. And they did not repent of their murders or of their sorceries or of their immorality or of their thefts.

And I saw another angel, a strong one, coming down from heaven, clothed in a cloud, and the rainbow was over his head, and his face was like the sun, and his feet like pillars of fire. And he had in his hand a little open scroll; and he set his right foot upon the sea but his left foot upon the earth. And he cried with a loud voice as when a lion roars. And when he had cried, the seven thunders spoke out their voices. And when the seven thunders had spoken, I was about to write; and I heard a voice from heaven saying, "Seal up the things that the seven thunders spoke, and do not write them."

And the angel whom I saw standing on the sea and on the earth, lifted up his hand to heaven, and swore by him who lives forever and ever, who created heaven and the things that are therein, and the earth and the things that are therein, and the sea and the things that are therein, and that there shall be delay no longer; but that in the days of the voice of the seventh angel, when he begins to sound the trumpet, the mystery of God will be accomplished, as he declared by his servants the prophets.

And the voice that I heard from heaven was speaking with me again, and saying, "Go, take the open scroll from the hand of the angel who stands upon the sea and upon the earth." And I went away to the angel, telling him to give me the scroll. And he said to me, "Take the scroll and eat it up, and it will make thy stomach bitter, but in thy mouth it will be sweet as honey." And I took the scroll from the angel's hand, and ate it up, and it was in my mouth sweet as honey, and when I had eaten it my stomach was made bitter. And they said to me, "Thou must prophesy again to many nations and peoples and tongues and kings."

And there was given me a reed like to a rod, and I was told: "Rise and measure the temple of God, and the altar and those who worship therein. But the court outside the temple, reject it, and do not measure it; for it has been given to the nations, and the holy city they will trample under foot for forty-two months. And I will grant unto my two witnesses to prophesy for a thousand two hundred and sixty days, clothed in sackcloth."

These are the two olive trees and the two lamp-stands that stand before the Lord of the earth. And if anyone desires to harm them, fire will come out of their mouths, and will devour their enemies. And if anyone desires to injure them, he must in this manner be killed. These have power to shut heaven, so that it will not rain during the days of their prophesying; and they have power over the waters to turn them into blood, and to smite the earth with every plague as often as they desire.

And when they have finished their testimony, the beast that comes up out of the abyss will wage war against them, and will conquer them and will kill them. And their dead bodies will lie in the streets of the great city, which is called mystically Sodom and Egypt, where their Lord also was crucified. And men from the tribes and peoples and tongues and nations will look upon their bodies three days and a half; and they will not allow their dead bodies to be laid in tombs. And the inhabitants of the earth will rejoice over them and make merry; and they will send gifts to one another because these two prophets tormented the inhabitants of the earth.

And after the three days and a half, the breath of life from God entered into them. And they stood up on their feet, and a great fear fell upon those who saw them. And they heard a great voice from heaven saying to them, "Come up hither." And they went up to heaven in a cloud, and their enemies saw them. And at that hour there was a great earthquake and the tenth part of the city fell; and there were killed in the earthquake seven thousand persons; and the rest were affrighted and gave glory to the God of heaven.

The second woe is past; and behold, the third woe will come quickly.

And the seventh angel sounded the trumpet; and there were loud voices in heaven saying, "The kingdom of this world has become the kingdom of our Lord and of his Christ, and he shall reign forever and ever." And the twenty-four elders who sit upon their thrones before God fell on their faces and worshipped God, saying, "We give thee thanks, O Lord God almighty, who art, and who wast, because thou hast taken thy great power and hast begun thy reign. And the nations were angered, but thy wrath came and the time for the dead to be judged, and for giving the reward to thy servants—the prophets, and the saints, and those who fear thy name, the small and the great—and for destroying those who corrupted the earth." And the temple of God in heaven was opened, and there was seen the ark of his covenant in his temple, and there came flashes of lightning, and peals of thunder, and an earthquake, and great hail.

IV. THE SEVEN SIGNS

And a great sign appeared in heaven: a woman clothed with the sun, and the moon was under her feet, and upon her head a crown of twelve stars. And being with child, she cried out in her travail and was in the anguish of delivery. And another sign was seen in heaven, and behold, a great red dragon having seven heads and ten horns, and upon his heads seven diadems. And his tail was dragging along the third part of the stars of heaven, and it dashed them to the earth; and the dragon stood before the woman who was about to bring forth, that when she had brought forth he might devour her son. And she brought forth a male child, who is to rule all nations with a rod of iron; and her child was caught up to God and to his throne. And the woman fled into the wilderness, where she has a place prepared by God, that there they may nourish her a thousand two hundred and sixty days.

And there was a battle in heaven; Michael and his angels battled with the dragon, and the dragon fought and his angels. And they did not prevail, neither was their place found any more in heaven. And that great dragon was cast down, the ancient serpent, he who is called the devil and Satan, who leads astray the whole world; and he was cast down to the earth and with him his angels were cast down.

And I heard a loud voice in heaven saying, "Now has come the salvation, and the power and the kingdom of our God, and the authority of his Christ; for the accuser of our brethren has been cast down, he who accused them before our God day and night. And they overcame him through the blood of the Lamb and through the word of their witness, for they did not love their lives even in face of death. There-fore rejoice, O heavens, and you who dwell therein. Woe to the earth and to the sea, because the devil has gone down to you in great wrath, knowing that he has but a short time."

And when the dragon saw that he was cast down to the earth, he pursued the woman who had brought forth the male child. And there were given to the woman the two wings of a great eagle, that she might fly into the wilderness unto her place, where she is nourished for a time and times and a half time, away from the serpent. And the serpent cast out of his mouth after the woman water like a river, that he might cause her to be carried away by the river. And the earth helped the woman, and the earth opened her mouth and swallowed up the river that the dragon had cast out of his mouth. And the dragon was angered at the woman, and went away to wage war with the rest of her offspring, who keep the commandments of God, and hold fast the testimony of Jesus. And he stood upon the sand of the sea.

And I saw a beast coming up out of the sea, having seven heads and ten horns, and upon its horns ten diadems, and upon its heads blasphemous names. And the beast that I saw was like a leopard, and its feet were like the feet of a bear, and its mouth like the mouth of a lion. And the dragon gave it his own might and authority. And one of its heads was smitten, as it were, unto death; but its deadly wound was healed. And all the earth followed the beast in wonder. And they worshipped the dragon because he gave authority to the beast, and they worshipped the beast, saying, "Who is like to the beast, and who will be able to fight with it?"

And there was given to it a mouth speaking great things and blasphemies; and there was given to it authority to work for forty-two months. And it opened its mouth for blasphemies against God, to blaspheme his name and his tabernacle, and those who dwell in heaven. And it was allowed to wage war with the saints and to overcome them. And there was given to it authority over every tribe, and people, and tongue, and nation. And all the inhabitants of the earth will worship it whose names have not been written in the book of life of the Lamb who has been slain from the foundation of the world.

If any man has an ear, let him hear. He who is for captivity, into captivity he goes; he who kills by the sword, by the sword must he be killed. Here is the patience and the faith of the saints.

And I saw another beast coming up out of the earth, and it had two horns like those of a lamb, but it spoke as does a dragon. And it exercised all the authority of the former beast in its sight; and it made the earth and the inhabitants therein to worship the first beast, whose deadly wound was healed. And it did great signs, so as even to make fire come down from heaven upon earth in the sight of mankind. And it leads astray the inhabitants of the earth, by reason of the signs which it was permitted to do in the sight of the beast, telling the inhabitants of the earth to make an image to the beast which has the wound of the sword, and yet lived. And it was permitted to give life to the image of the beast, that the image of the beast should both speak and cause that whoever should not worship the image of the beast should be killed. And it will cause all, the small and the great, and the rich and the poor, and the free and the bond, to have a mark on their right hand or on their foreheads, and it will bring it about that no one may be able to buy or sell, except him who has the mark, either the name of the beast or the number of its name.

Here is wisdom. He who has understanding, let him calculate the number of the beast, for it is the number of a man; and its number is six hundred and sixty-six.

And I saw, and behold, the Lamb was standing upon Mount Sion, and with him a hundred and forty-four thousand having his name and the name of his Father written on their foreheads. And I heard a voice from heaven like a voice of many waters, and like a voice of loud thunder; and the voice that I heard was as of harpers playing their harps. And they were singing as it were a new song before the throne, and before the four living creatures and the elders; and no one could learn the song except those hundred and forty-four thousand, who have been purchased from the earth. These are they who were not defiled with women; for they are virgins. These follow the Lamb wherever he goes. These were purchased from among men, first-fruits unto God and unto the Lamb, and in their mouth there was found no lie; they are without blemish.

And I saw another angel flying in midheaven, having an everlasting gospel to preach to those who dwell upon the earth and to every nation and tribe and tongue and people, saying with a loud voice, "Fear God, and give him honor, for the hour of his judgment has come; and worship him who made the heaven and the earth, the sea and the fountains of waters." And another angel followed, saying, "She has fallen, Babylon the great, who of the wine of the wrath of her immorality has given all the nations to drink."

And another, a third angel followed them, saying with a loud voice, "If anyone worships the beast and its image and receives a mark upon his forehead or upon his right hand, he also shall drink of the wine of the wrath of God, which is poured unmixed into the cup of his wrath; and he shall be tormented with fire and brimstone in the sight of the holy angels and in the sight of the Lamb. And the smoke of their torments goes up forever and ever; and they rest neither day nor night, they who have worshipped the beast and its image, and anyone who receives the mark of its name."

Here is the patience of the saints, who keep the commandments of God, and the faith of Jesus. And I heard a voice from heaven saying, "Write: Blessed are the dead who die in the Lord henceforth. Yes, says the Spirit, let them rest from their labors, for their works follow them."

And I saw, and behold, a white cloud, and upon the cloud one sitting like to a son of man, having upon his head a crown of gold and in his hand a sharp sickle. And another angel came forth out of the temple crying with a loud voice to him who sat upon the cloud, "Put forth thy sickle and reap, for the hour to reap has come, because the harvest of the earth is ripe." And he who sat on the cloud cast his sickle upon the earth, and the earth was reaped.

And another angel came forth out of the temple that is in heaven, he also having a sharp sickle. And another angel came forth from the altar, he who has authority over the fire, and he called with a loud voice to him who had the sharp sickle, saying, "Put forth thy sharp sickle and gather the clusters of the vine of the earth; for its grapes are fully ripe." And the angel cast his sickle to the earth, and gathered the vintage of the earth, and cast it into the great wine press of the wrath of God. And the wine press was trodden outside the city, and there came forth blood out of the wine press, up to the horses' bridles, for a thousand and six hundred stadia.

And I saw another sign in heaven, great and marvellous, seven angels having the seven last plagues. For in them has been completed the wrath of God.

And I saw as it were a sea of glass mingled with fire, and those who had overcome the beast and its image and the number of its name, standing on the sea of glass, having the harps of God and singing the song of Moses, the servant of God, and the song of the Lamb, saying, "Great and marvellous are thy works, O Lord God almighty; just and true are thy ways, O King of the ages. Who will not fear thee, O Lord, and magnify thy name? for thou alone art holy. For all nations will come and worship before thee; because thy judgments are manifest."

V. THE SEVEN BOWLS

And after this I looked, and behold, the temple of the tabernacle of the testimony was opened in heaven, and there came forth out of the temple the seven angels who had the seven plagues, clothed with clean white linen, and girt about their breasts with golden girdles. And one of the four living creatures gave to the seven angels seven golden bowls, full of the wrath of God who lives forever and ever. And the temple was filled with smoke from the majesty of God, and from his power; and no one could enter into the temple till the seven plagues of the seven angels were finished.

And I heard a loud voice from the temple saying to the seven angels, "Go and pour out the seven bowls of the wrath of God upon the earth." And the first went and poured out his bowl upon the earth, and a sore and grievous wound was made upon the men who have the mark of the beast, and upon those who worshipped its image. And the second poured out his bowl upon the sea, and it became blood as of a dead man; and every live thing in the sea died. And the third poured out his bowl upon the rivers and fountains of waters, and they became blood.

And I heard the angel of the waters saying, "Thou art just, O Lord, who art and who wast, O Holy One, because thou hast judged these things; because they poured out the blood of saints and prophets, blood also thou hast given them to drink; they deserve it!" And I heard the altar saying, "Yes, O Lord God almighty, true and just are thy judgments."

And the fourth poured out his bowl upon the sun, and he was allowed to scorch mankind with fire. And mankind were scorched with great heat, and they blasphemed the name of God who has authority over these plagues, and they did not repent and give him glory. And the fifth poured out his bowl upon the throne of the beast; and its kingdom became dark, and they gnawed their tongues for pain. And they blasphemed the God of heaven because of their pains and their wounds, and they did not repent of their works. And the sixth poured out his bowl upon the great river Euphrates, and dried up its waters, that a way might be made ready for the kings from the rising sun.

And I saw issuing from the mouth of the dragon, and from the mouth of the beast, and from the mouth of the false prophet, three unclean spirits like frogs. For they are spirits of demons working signs, and they go forth unto the kings of the whole earth to gather them together for the battle on the great day of God almighty. "Behold, I come as a thief! Blessed is he who watches and keeps his garments, lest he walk naked and they see his shame." And he gathered them together in a place that is called in Hebrew Armagedon.

And the seventh poured out his bowl upon the air, and there came forth a loud voice out of the temple from the throne, saying, "It has come to pass!" And there were flashes of lightning, rumblings and peals of thunder, and there was a great earthquake such as never has been since men were first upon the earth, so great an earthquake was it. And the great city came into three parts; and the cities of the nations fell. And Babylon the great was remembered before God, to give her the cup of the wine of his fierce wrath. And every island fled away, and the mountains could not be found. And great hail, heavy as a talent, came down from heaven upon men; and men blasphemed God because of the plague of hail; for it was very great.

VI. BABYLON THE GREAT

And there came one of the seven angels who had the seven bowls, and he spoke to me, saying, "Come, I will show thee the condemnation of the great harlot who sits upon many waters, with whom the kings of the earth have committed fornication, and the inhabitants of the earth were made drunk with the wine of her immorality."

And he took me away in spirit into a desert. And I saw a woman sitting upon a scarlet-colored beast, full of names of blasphemy, having seven heads and ten horns. And the woman was clothed in purple and scarlet, and covered with gold and precious stones and pearls, having in her hand a golden cup full of abominations and the uncleanness of her immorality. And upon her forehead a name written—a mystery—Babylon the great, mother of the harlotries and of the abominations of the earth. And I saw the woman drunk with the blood of the saints and with the blood of the martyrs of Jesus. And when I saw her, I wondered with a great wonder.

And the angel said to me, "Wherefore dost thou wonder? I will tell thee the mystery of the woman, and of the beast that carries her which has the seven heads and the ten horns. The beast that thou sawest was, and is not, and is about to come up from the abyss, and will go to destruction. And the inhabitants of the earth—whose names have not been written in the book of life from the foundation of the world—will wonder when they see the beast which was, and is not. And here is the meaning for him who has wisdom. The seven heads are seven mountains upon which the woman sits; and they are seven kings; five of them have fallen, one is, and the other has not yet come; and when he comes, he must remain a short time. And the beast that was, and is not, is moreover himself eighth, and is of the seven, and is on his way to destruction.

"And the ten horns that thou sawest are ten kings, who have not received a kingdom as yet, but they will receive authority as kings for one hour with the beast. These have one purpose, and their power and authority they give to the beast. These will fight with the Lamb, and the Lamb will overcome them, for he is the Lord of lords, and the King of kings, and they who are with him, called, and chosen, and faithful."

And he said to me, "The waters that thou sawest where

the harlot sits, are peoples and nations and tongues. And the ten horns that thou sawest, and the beast, these will hate the harlot, and will make her desolate and naked, and will eat her flesh, and will burn her up in fire. For God has put it into their hearts to carry out his purpose, to give their kingdom to the beast, until the words of God are accomplished. And the woman whom thou sawest is the great city which has kingship over the kings of the earth."

And after this I saw another angel coming down from heaven, having great authority, and the earth was lighted up by his glory. And he cried out with a mighty voice, saying, "She has fallen, she has fallen, Babylon the great; and has become a habitation of demons, a stronghold of every unclean spirit, a stronghold of every unclean and hateful bird; because all the nations have drunk of the wrath of her immorality, and the kings of the earth have committed fornication with her, and by the power of her wantonness the merchants of the earth have grown rich."

And I heard another voice from heaven saying, "Go out from her, my people, that you may not share in her sins, and that you may not receive of her plagues. For her sins have reached even to heaven, and the Lord has remembered her iniquities. Render to her as she also has rendered, and give her the double according to her works; in the cup that she has mixed, mix for her double. As much as she glorified herself and gave herself to wantonness, so much torment and mourning give to her. Because in her heart she says, 'I sit a queen, I am no widow, and I shall not see mourning.' Therefore in one day her plagues shall come, death and mourning and famine; and she shall be burnt up in fire; for strong is God who will judge her."

And the kings of the earth who with her committed fornication and lived wantonly will weep and mourn over her
when they see the smoke of her burning, standing afar off
for fear of her torments, saying, "Woe, woe, the great city,
Babylon, the strong city, for in one hour has thy judgment
come!"

And the merchants of the earth will weep and mourn
over her; for no one will buy their merchandise any more:
merchandise of gold and silver, and precious stones and
pearls, and fine linen and purple, and silk and scarlet, and
all thyine wood, and all vessels of ivory, and all vessels of
precious stone, and of brass, and of iron, and of marble,
and cinnamon and amomum and spices, and ointment and
frankincense, and wine and oil, and fine flour and wheat,
and beasts of burden and sheep and horses, and chariots
and slaves, and souls of men. And the fruit which was the
desire of thy soul departed from thee; and all the fat and
splendid things perished from thee, and men will find them
nevermore. The merchants of these things, who grew rich by
her, will stand afar off for fear of her torments, weeping and
mourning, and saying, "Woe, woe, the great city, which was
clothed in fine linen and purple and scarlet, and gilded in
gold, and precious stone, and pearls; for in one hour riches
so great were laid waste!"

And every shipmaster, and everyone who sails to a place,
and mariners, and all who work upon the sea, stood afar off,
and cried out as they saw the place of her burning, saying,
"What city is like to this great city?" And they cast dust on
their heads, and cried out weeping and mourning, saying,
"Woe, woe, the great city, wherein all who had their ships
at sea were made rich out of her wealth; for in one hour she

has been laid waste!" Make merry over her, O heaven, and you the saints and the apostles and the prophets, for God has judged your cause upon her.

And a strong angel took up a stone, as it were a great millstone, and cast it into the sea, saying, "With this violence will Babylon, the great city, be overthrown, and will not be found any more. And the sound of harpers and musicians and flute-players and trumpet will not be heard in thee any more; and no craftsman of any craft will be found in thee any more; and sound of millstone will not be heard in thee any more. And light of lamp will not shine in thee any more; and voice of bridegroom and of bride will not be heard in thee any more; because thy merchants were the great men of the earth, for by thy sorcery all the nations have been led astray. And in her was found blood of prophets and of saints, and of all who have been slain upon the earth."

After these things I heard as it were a loud voice of a great crowd in heaven, saying, "Alleluia! salvation and glory and power belong to our God. For true and just are his judgments, who has judged the great harlot who corrupted the earth with her fornication, and has avenged the blood of his servants at her hands." And again they have said, "Alleluia! And the smoke of her goes up forever and ever!" And the twenty-four elders and the four living creatures fell down and worshipped God who sits on the throne, and they said, "Amen! Alleluia!" And a voice came forth from the throne, saying, "Praise our God, all you his servants, and you who fear him, the small and the great!"

And I heard as it were a voice of a great crowd, and as the voice of many waters, and as the voice of mighty thunders, saying, "Alleluia! for the Lord, our God almighty, now reigns! Let us be glad and rejoice, and give glory to him; for the marriage of the Lamb has come, and his spouse has prepared herself. And she has been permitted to clothe herself in fine linen, shining, bright. For the fine linen is the just deeds of the saints."

And he said to me, "Write: Blessed are they who are called to the marriage supper of the Lamb." And he said to me, "These are true words of God." And I fell down before his feet to worship him. And he said to me, "Thou must not do that. I am a fellow-servant of thine and of thy brethren who give testimony of Jesus. Worship God! for the testimony of Jesus is the spirit of prophecy."

VII. THE CONSUMMATION

And I saw heaven standing open; and behold, a white horse, and he who sat upon it is called Faithful and True, and with justice he judges and wages war. And his eyes are as a flame of fire, and on his head are many diadems; he has a name written which no man knows except himself. And he is clothed in a garment sprinkled with blood, and his name is called The Word of God. And the armies of heaven, clothed in fine linen, white and pure, were following him on white horses.

And from his mouth goes forth a sharp sword with which to smite the nations. And he will rule them with a rod of iron, and he treads the wine press of the fierce wrath of God almighty. And he has on his garment and on his thigh a name written, "King of kings and Lord of lords."

And I saw an angel standing in the sun, and he cried with

a loud voice, saying to all the birds that fly in midheaven, "Come, gather yourselves together to the great supper of God, that you may eat flesh of kings, and flesh of tribunes, and flesh of mighty men, and flesh of horses, and of those who sit upon them, and flesh of all men, free and bond, small and great."

And I saw the beast, and the kings of the earth and their armies gathered to wage war against him who was sitting upon the horse, and against his army. And the beast was seized, and with it the false prophet who did signs before it wherewith he deceived those who accepted the mark of the beast and who worshipped its image. These two were cast alive into the pool of fire that burns with brimstone. And the rest were killed with the sword of him who sits upon the horse, the sword that goes forth out of his mouth; and all the birds were filled with their flesh.

And I saw an angel coming down from heaven, having the key of the abyss and a great chain in his hand. And he laid hold on the dragon, the ancient serpent, who is the devil and Satan, and bound him for a thousand years. And he cast him into the abyss, and closed and sealed it over him, that he should deceive the nations no more, until the thousand years should be finished. And after that he must be let loose for a little while.

And I saw thrones, and men sat upon them and judgment was given to them. And I saw the souls of those who had been beheaded because of the witness to Jesus and because of the word of God, and who did not worship the beast or his image, and did not accept his mark upon their foreheads or upon their hands. And they came to life and reigned with Christ a thousand years. The rest of the dead did not come to life till the thousand years were finished. This is the first resurrection. Blessed and holy is he who has part in the first resurrection! Over these the second death has no power; but they will be priests of God and Christ, and will reign with him a thousand years.

And when the thousand years are finished, Satan will be released from his prison, and will go forth and deceive the nations which are in the four corners of the earth, Gog and Magog, and will gather them together for the battle; the number of whom is as the sand of the sea. And they went up over the breadth of the earth and encompassed the camp of the saints, and the beloved city. And fire from God came down out of heaven and devoured them. And the devil who deceived them was cast into the pool of fire and brimstone, where are also the beast and the false prophet; and they will be tormented day and night forever and ever.

And I saw a great white throne and the one who sat upon it; from his face the earth and heaven fled away, and there was found no place for them. And I saw the dead, the great and the small, standing before the throne, and scrolls were opened. And another scroll was opened, which is the book of life; and the dead were judged out of those things that were written in the scrolls, according to their works. And the sea gave up the dead that were in it, and death and hell gave up the dead that were in them; and they were judged each one, according to their works.

And hell and death were cast into the pool of fire. This is the second death, the pool of fire. And if anyone was not found written in the book of life, he was cast into the pool of fire.

And I saw a new heaven and a new earth. For the first

heaven and the first earth passed away, and the sea is no more. And I saw the holy city, New Jerusalem, coming down out of heaven from God, made ready as a bride adorned for her husband. And I heard a loud voice from the throne saying, "Behold the dwelling of God with men, and he will dwell with them. And they will be his people, and God himself will be with them as their God. And God will wipe away every tear from their eyes. And death shall be no more; neither shall there be mourning, nor crying, nor pain any more, for the former things have passed away."

And he who was sitting on the throne said, "Behold, I make all things new!" And he said, "Write, for these words are trustworthy and true." And he said to me, "It is done! I am the Alpha and the Omega, the beginning and the end. To him who thirsts I will give of the fountain of the water of life freely. He who overcomes shall possess these things, and I will be his God, and he shall be my son. But as for the cowardly and unbelieving, and abominable and murderers, and fornicators and sorcerers, and idolaters and all liars, their portion shall be in the pool that burns with fire and brimstone, which is the second death."

And there came one of the seven angels who had the bowls full of the seven last plagues; and he spoke with me, saying, "Come, I will show thee the bride, the spouse of the Lamb." And he took me up in spirit to a mountain, great and high, and showed me the holy city Jerusalem, coming down out of heaven from God, having the glory of God. Its light was like to a precious stone, as it were a jasper-stone, clear as crystal. And it had a wall great and high with twelve gates, and at the gates twelve angels, and names written on them, which are the names of the twelve tribes of the children of

Israel. On the east are three gates, and on the north three gates, and on the south three gates, and on the west three gates. And the wall of the city has twelve foundation stones, and on them twelve names of the twelve apostles of the Lamb.

And he who spoke with me had a measure, a golden reed, to measure the city and the gates thereof and the wall. And the city stands foursquare, and its length is as great as its breadth; and he measured the city with the reed, to twelve thousand stadia: the length and the breadth and the height of it are equal. And he measured its wall, of a hundred and forty-four cubits, man's measure, that is, angel's measure. And the material of its wall was jasper; but the city itself was pure gold, like pure glass. And the foundations of the wall of the city were adorned with every precious stone. The first foundation, jasper; the second, sapphire; the third, agate; the fourth, emerald; the fifth, sardonyx; the sixth, sardius; the seventh, chrysolite; the eighth, beryl; the ninth, topaz; the tenth, chrysoprase; the eleventh, jacinth; the twelfth, amethyst. And the twelve gates were twelve pearls; that is, each gate was of a single pearl. And the street of the city was pure gold, as it were transparent glass.

And I saw no temple therein. For the Lord God almighty and the Lamb are the temple thereof. And the city has no need of the sun or the moon to shine upon it. For the glory of God lights it up, and the Lamb is the lamp thereof. And the nations shall walk by the light thereof; and the kings of the earth shall bring their glory and honor into it. And its gates shall not be shut by day; for there shall be no night there. And they shall bring the glory and the honor of the nations into it. And there shall not enter into it anything undefiled, nor he who practises abomination and falsehood, but those only who are written in the book of life of the Lamb.

And he showed me a river of the water of life, clear as crystal, coming forth from the throne of God and of the Lamb. In the midst of the city street, on both sides of the river, was the tree of life, bearing twelve fruits, yielding its fruit according to each month, and the leaves for the healing of the nations.

And there shall be no more any accursed thing; but the throne of God and of the Lamb shall be in it, and his servants shall serve him. And they shall see his face and his name shall be on their foreheads. And night shall be no more, and they shall have no need of light of lamp, or light of sun, for the Lord God will shed light upon them; and they shall reign forever and ever.

EPILOGUE

And he said to me, "These words are trustworthy and true; and the Lord, the God of the spirits of the prophets, sent his angel to show to his servants what must shortly come to pass. And behold, I come quickly! Blessed is he who keeps the words of the prophecy of this book." And I, John, am he who heard and saw these things. And when I heard and saw, I fell down to worship at the feet of the angel who showed me these things. And he said to me, "Thou must not do that. I am a fellow-servant of thine and of thy brethren the prophets, and of those who keep the words of this book. Worship God!"

And he said to me, "Do not seal up the words of the prophecy of this book; for the time is at hand. He who does wrong, let him do wrong still; and he who is filthy, let him be filthy still; and he who is just, let him be just still; and he who is holy, let him be hallowed still. Behold, I come quickly! And my reward is with me, to render to each one according to his works. I am the Alpha and Omega, the first and the last, the beginning and the end!" Blessed are they who wash their robes that they may enter into the city. Outside are the dogs, and the sorcerers, and the fornicators, and the murderers and the idolaters, and everyone who loves and practises falsehood.

"I, Jesus, have sent my angel to testify to you these things concerning the churches. I am the root and the offspring of David, the bright morning star." And the Spirit and the bride say, "Come!" And let him who hears say, "Come!" And let him who thirsts come; and he who wishes, let him receive the water of life freely. I testify to everyone who hears the words of the prophecy of this book. If anyone shall add to them, God will add unto him the plagues that are written in this book. And if anyone shall take away from the words of the book of this prophecy, God will take away his portion from the tree of life, and from the holy city, and from the things that are written in this book. He who testifies to these things says, "It is true, I come quickly!" Amen! Come, Lord Jesus! The grace of our Lord Jesus Christ be with all. Amen.

Sophia Institute

Sophia Institute is a nonprofit institution that seeks to nurture the spiritual, moral, and cultural life of souls and to spread the Gospel of Christ in conformity with the authentic teachings of the Roman Catholic Church.

Sophia Institute Press fulfills this mission by offering translations, reprints, and new publications that afford readers a rich source of the enduring wisdom of mankind.

Sophia Institute also operates the popular online resource CatholicExchange.com. *Catholic Exchange* provides world news from a Catholic perspective as well as daily devotionals and articles that will help readers to grow in holiness and live a life consistent with the teachings of the Church.

In 2013, Sophia Institute launched Sophia Institute for Teachers to renew and rebuild Catholic culture through service to Catholic education. With the goal of nurturing the spiritual, moral, and cultural life of souls, and an abiding respect for the role and work of teachers, we strive to provide materials and programs that are at once enlightening to the mind and ennobling to the heart; faithful and complete, as well as useful and practical.

Sophia Institute gratefully recognizes the Solidarity Association for preserving and encouraging the growth of our apostolate over the course of many years. Without their generous and timely support, this book would not be in your hands.

www.SophiaInstitute.com
www.CatholicExchange.com
www.SophiaInstituteforTeachers.org